shift

HELPING CONGREGATIONS BACK INTO THE GAME OF EFFECTIVE MINISTRY

DR. PHIL MAYNARD

Paperback ISBN 978-0-9899223-0-2

Ebook ISBN 978-9899-223-1-9

Printed in USA

Dedication

"No book gets written in a vacuum. Certainly not this one. Many people have provided insights into the best practices included in these materials. Dozens of congregations have engaged processes of learning and development willingly providing a laboratory for discovering what works and what does not. My thanks to all.

But most of all I want to thank my wife Becky who has been such a great source of encouragement, support, accountability, and persistence. This book is better because of her attention to detail. And so am I."

"Intentionality"
Rev. Phil Maynard

Table of Contents

FOREWORD TO *SHIFT*

I have consulted with hundreds of churches in the last few years—and so it is no small thing for me to say that *Shift* is relevant to every single one of those churches. *All* of them. This is the first book I have run across in some time about which I can say this.

When my colleague Phil Maynard first told me about the manuscript he was writing (in a Popeye's Restaurant in Jacksonville, Florida earlier this year), I listened carefully to the five major shifts that he was proposing. I told him, "You nailed it. Those *are* the shifts." In an era where everyone has a different angle and prescription for how to fix ailing churches, rarely do we see a resource that really cuts to the bottom line. Phil has identified the key shifts that all churches must make if they are to have a fruitful ministry in the next decade. Rural, urban, black, Hispanic, Anglo, Asian, multicultural, liberal, evangelical—they all need to think through these key shifts, and figure out a path forward in ministry in sync with each.

When I finally got my hands on the manuscript and started reading, the first thing that went through my mind was not some floundering church with which I am consulting, but rather the new church launch team with which I am working in my home town. In other words, the key concepts and practices outlined in *Shift* are just as relevant to a brand-new church as to a church that is seeking to renew its ministry. The reason for this is because so often the leaders in new churches bring along baggage from the twentieth-century church.

A few of you may lead missional churches—and you may totally get the shift from Serve-us to Service. But my coaching group works with enough missional churches to know that most of them have to work constantly at moving forward in terms of biblical hospitality and calling people to depth of discipleship.

You may think your church has its act together and does not need any coaching. Careful there! For many effective churches, Phil Maynard's suggested shifts will unpack and bring clarity to key shifts they have already made. Nonetheless, all growing churches constantly experience the temptation to get lazy because their ministry is thriving. When we get lazy, we tend to fall back into old habits and ways of thinking.

Most twenty-first century churches, however, are neither new nor missional nor effective in reaching people with the gospel. That's just the truth of the matter. Most of our churches are stuck, declining, aging and struggling in various ways. *Shift* is written most explicitly for the church that thought they had ministry figured out 30 years ago, but where nothing today is working as well as it used to work. If this is the case in the place that you call church, I encourage you to buy up a box full of copies of *Shift* and to get your church's leaders thinking through each of these key movements.

It would not hurt for all of your church's leaders to read the whole book. But then you can divide it up by areas of ministry responsibility and invite one group to really dig into the chapter on hospitality (which, I might add, is the best and most comprehensive thing I have read on that subject since I picked up a copy of Nouwen's *Reaching Out* in 1979). Another group, that leads worship, can dig into that chapter. And so forth. I cannot imagine any ministry team wasting their time on this—the discussions, the ah-ha's, the practical improvements to ministry are almost guaranteed to any ministry team that seriously engages *Shift*!

Thank you, Phil Maynard, for giving us this immensely practical book—as we dig into its pages, you provide us more than good theory: you coach us and suggest to us excellent resources. I celebrate all of the shifts that are about to speed up in churches all over North America because they get their hands on these pages.

—*Paul Nixon*

Author of several popular books, including *We Refuse to Lead a Dying Church* and *The Surprise Factor*

Leader of two organizations: Epicenter Group and Readiness 360

National Consultant and Coach for congregations in redevelopment and for new church plants

New Church Strategist for Path 1 (New Church Start Division of the General Board of Discipleship, United Methodist Church)

Introduction

Picture the scene in Ezekiel 37. Imagine God in a valley leading the prophet back and forth among broken, brittle bones—a place no Jew wants to be. Then God asks, "Can these bones live?" The situation must have looked hopeless to Ezekiel, but he replies, "Sovereign LORD, you alone know." Then God commands him to prophesy to the bones and, when he obeys, a miracle occurs. It starts as a noise, a rattling sound, as the bones come together. God attaches the tendons and then covers the skeletons with skin. Then from the four winds, God breathes life into those dry bones and they stand on their feet, ready to occupy the land and be a force for God.

While Ezekiel's vision was intended to bring hope to the Jewish exiles following their capture by King Nebuchadnezzar of Babylon, that Scripture passage is still a powerful image today. It is a reminder of God's power to restore.

Look around you. Where are you seeing the fresh wind of God's Spirit breathe new life into dry, brittle bones?

As a church consultant and denominational leader, I am witnessing God breathe new life into churches with whom I have worked. Congregations are making the Shift—actually a series of individual shifts that, when combined together, shift the culture of their churches—bringing vitality and fruitfulness. These individual shifts include:

- From *Fellowship* to *Hospitality*
- From *Worship as an Event* to *Worship as a Lifestyle*
- From *Membership* to *Discipleship*
- From *"Serve Us"* to *Service*
- From *"Survival Mentality"* to *Generosity*

I am writing this book because I believe that every church has the potential to be vital and fruitful. These are not just buzzwords. They are words filled with hope and promise.

Not every church will choose to live into this potential.

We all know of churches that have made the decision to circle the wagons, hang on to their revered traditions, focus on the contentment of 'members,' and ignore the world around them. If this is your church, or a church you are working with or trying to coach to health, this material may not be for you.

But if the church has the will to move into a more vital ministry, this material is full of great ideas to help you do that. It is not easy. This Shift will require much of you. It will challenge some of your long-held assumptions about what effective ministry looks like. It will require letting go of some things that may have been held dear for a lifetime. And it will engage the most creative parts of your being to apply clear principles to your context.

Every church will need to take the concepts, tools, and practices and figure out how they best work in its particular context. Questions have been provided to help leaders and coaches lead their congregations in meaningful conversation about where they are and where they want to go.

shift 1:

From Fellowship to Hospitality

"My command is this: Love each other as I have loved you."
Jesus, John 15:12

"Life is not about stuff we own or accumulate. It is not even about personal accomplishment. Life is about people. We can replace stuff, but we can't replace people!"
Michael Slaughter, *Momentum for Life*[1]

"As a school for love, the church becomes a congregation where people learn from one another how to love."
Bishop Robert Schnase, *Five Practices of Fruitful Congregations*[2]

Consider the following. ...It's a familiar story lived out in many congregations across the United States.

Someone is in crisis, a couple has their first child, or a family moves to the area. They decide to attend the church down the street. They don't know anyone, so they arrive late and slip into the back row of seats. Because the bulletin is geared to the congregation, they struggle to keep up with what is going on. During "moments of friendliness," a few people nod at them but most of the congregation visits with each other. After the service, someone points them in the direction of the Fellowship Hall where there is coffee, but then leaves them. When they go, they end up standing there on their own. It would be no different if they attended a small group or Sunday school class. The people in the church have known each other so long that it would be difficult to break in. They don't know the stories, the history, the people.

How do you react to this story? How does it make you feel? No wonder so few are coming to know the love of Jesus! People are not seeing it lived out, even in the one place that they would expect to find it.

13

Observations about Hospitality

Hospitality is more than fellowship with one another. It's about opening our hearts to others and building relationships, plain and simple. Let's consider some observations about hospitality in the local congregation based on current research and my work with congregations in transformation:

- Depending on the study referenced, somewhere between 60–80% of people who visit a congregation come because they were personally invited.

- As a general rule, in most communities, 50% or less of the population is participating in the life of any congregation.

- Most people who visit a congregation decide within the first 10 minutes or less following arrival on the church campus whether or not they will return. This, of course, is long before the pastor preaches and sometimes even before the music starts!

- The driving factor in the decision to return is often the personal connections made by members of the congregation—not the greeters or pastor.

- People are more engaged in the life of the congregation if they have a good friend who is also involved.

- The follow-up with first-time visitors and with those who have missed a couple of consecutive weeks in worship is a key factor in maintaining the relationship.

- Hospitality is a significant dimension of Christian discipleship and can be developed through intentional discipleship training.

- Hospitality is bigger than how one is welcomed to the worship event. It is part of a larger system of discipleship that includes friendships, intentional discipleship relationships, witnessing, and more.

- Hospitality includes both personal and congregational dimensions, and they are interrelated. Each supports the other.

When coaching the local congregation in the area of hospitality, all of these observations come into play. The goal is to help the congregation consider how to increase the relational level of its ministry. But perhaps the first question to consider is why this is even important from a theological perspective.

A Theology of Hospitality

Before we dig too deeply into the practical matters of moving toward excellence in the ways we offer hospitality, it needs to be clear why the shift from fellowship to hospitality is so important. Why are we to practice hospitality from a theological perspective? Isn't it enough that we gather with people who are like us and whom we like? Aren't we called to love each other, care for each other, and enjoy each other?

The Bible is pretty clear that this isn't enough!

In fact, from the charge of Abram: "I will bless you...and you will be a blessing...and all peoples on earth will be blessed through you (Genesis 12:2–3), to the charge from Jesus to "go and make disciples of all nations, baptizing them...and teaching them...(Matthew 28:19–20), to the vision offered John in Revelation that "they will be his people, and God himself will be with them and be their God...the old order of things has passed away...I am making everything new" (Revelation 21: 3–5), it is clear that the work of God is not limited to the fellowship of existing believers.

While hospitality in our contemporary culture has taken the form of 'fellowship' where we welcome friends to our table, in the biblical tradition hospitality was focused on welcoming the stranger. This includes those with the physical needs of shelter and nourishment but also those who know the pain of exclusion. Jesus himself modeled this as those who turned to him found welcome and the promise of being included in the Kingdom of God. Not only did he urge his followers to generously welcome those in need, but he also promised that these acts of kindness were personally experienced by the Son of Man himself (Matthew 25).

It's not just about us!

The driving force behind the building of relationships is the expression of God's grace (unmerited love) through the acceptance of all persons as being those God loves and the invitation for all to discover the fullness of that love for themselves. It is a grace that flows from the center of our experience of God's grace and extends to all peoples. People are accepted wherever they are in the flow of God's love and invited to discover the depths of God's love through the growth of relationships with other believers and the growth of a personal relationship with Jesus Christ.

We love because we have been loved. We welcome others because we have been welcomed. We invite others to discover this grace because of what we have learned about this transforming power of God's love.

This relational dimension is the engine that drives our witness in the community and world, our worship as the body of Christ, and our growth in maturity as disciples of Jesus Christ.

Let's consider a simple diagram to explain the 'big picture' approach to hospitality:

Dimensions of Hospitality

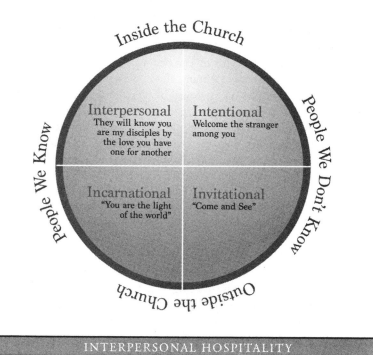

INTERPERSONAL HOSPITALITY

Refers to the level and quality of relational connections within the congregation, the people we know.

Key to all the dimensions of hospitality is that of Interpersonal Hospitality. This is all about meaningful connections at all points in the discipleship flow of a congregation. For example, I worked with a congregation that had been in crisis mode due to conflict between members and between members and the pastor for a couple of years. The tension in any gathering of the congregation (including worship) was so thick you could cut it with a knife. The amazing thing to me was that this congregation couldn't understand why people who showed up for worship in their beautiful 100-year-old sanctuary didn't seem to ever come back!

How we treat each other also shows up in the way others perceive our connection with them.

At the heart of the Christian faith journey is the idea of authentic relationships.

- We are called to be in relationship with God (Father, Son, and Holy Spirit)
- We are called to be in relationship with each other (modeling the relationship in which our Trinitarian God lives)
- We are called to be in relationship with those outside of the church

Graphically, these concepts are represented by three parts of the same whole:

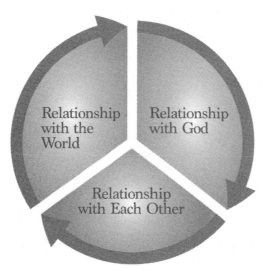

As each portion is strengthened, so is the next and so also is the whole.

I want to suggest five benefits of strong interpersonal hospitality:

- Synergy: power and energy that comes from spiritual friendships
- Motivation: challenge and influence to keep growing
- Encouragement: bringing comfort, consolation, and counsel to one another
- Accountability: objective counsel and helpful challenge
- Support: people to come alongside and help us keep going

In John 17:20–23, Jesus offers this prayer for believers:

I pray also for those who will believe in me through their message, that all of them may be one, Father, just as you are in me and I am in you. May they also be in us so that the world may believe that you have sent me. I have given them the glory that you gave me, that they may be one as we are one—I in them and you in me—so that they may be brought to complete unity. Then the world will know that you sent me and have loved them even as you have loved me.

There are several themes present in just these three verses. For example:

1. that to "be one, just as you are in me and I am in you" reflects on the unity of the Trinity,

2. that as we grow in relationship with God ("be in us"), the world will come to believe in Jesus,

3. that we (believers) can in fact become one with each other as fully as the Trinity is one,

4. that it is Jesus' prayer that we experience unity as believers, and

5. that our witness to the world depends on the kind of relationships we build.

Some practical considerations when it comes to living in authentic relationship with each other as disciples of Jesus include:

Forgiveness: Jesus said, "Blessed are the peacemakers" (Matthew 5:9). Paul said, "As far as it depends on you, live at peace with everyone" (Romans 12:18). How do you relate to people with whom you do not agree or who have hurt you? Jesus said that even sinners are nice to those who like and affirm them. "Love your enemies" (Matthew 5:44). "Bless those who curse you, pray for those who mistreat you" (Luke 6:28). Make peace with those who have hurt you. Our culture is strong on individual rights, on stressing what we deserve, and on what we are entitled to in relationships. Jesus turned much of this upside down and said to those for whom he died 'while we were yet sinners,' "Love each other as I have loved you" (John 15:12).

Acceptance: How do you relate to and welcome those who are different from you? In nature, "birds of a feather flock together."

But in the Kingdom of God, everyone is welcomed. This was hard for the early church to hear. The Holy Spirit expanded the early church's understanding of the inclusiveness of the Kingdom story by story, as if a bulldozer were knocking down every cultural barrier that kept people apart. Could sinners be welcomed? Could tax collectors and prostitutes? Could Greek-speaking Jews? Could Gentile God-fearers? Could Roman soldiers? Could godless Gentiles? Could those who had been worshiping foreign gods? The answer repeatedly was, "yes!" God's welcome includes even them. And the early church struggled to welcome all these different people into their table fellowship. Who might not feel welcomed by you into your small group or kneeling beside you taking communion? Jesus seemed purposefully to hang out with people who were not like him. What's more, they seemed to be drawn to his company. When you hang out with people not like you, are they drawn to you?

Accountability: The Apostle Paul scatters throughout his letters the "one anothers" that provide insight into how we are to do life together. A central theme in these "one anothers" is that of accountability, expressed in a variety of ways: submit to one another, encourage one another, admonish one another, bear with one another, agree with one another, live in harmony with one another, to name a few. Life as a disciple of Jesus Christ is lived in accountable relationships. This idea is also at the heart of the Methodist Movement begun by John Wesley. Community and authentic relationships were supported through class meetings by a high level of accountability using a Covenant of Discipleship.

Congregations that develop a strong sense of interpersonal hospitality help create safe places and safe people. Unlike "abandoners" who start a relationship but can't finish it; "critics" who take on a parental role, telling others what to do; or "irresponsibles" who don't take care of themselves or follow through on their commitments, safe people are trustworthy. In their book, *Safe People,* Cloud and Townsend describe a safe relationship as one that does three things:

- Draws us closer to God (Matthew 22:37–38)
- Draws us closer to others (Matthew 22:39)
- Helps us become the real person God created us to be (Ephesians 2:10).[3]

The following are some suggestions for developing safe places and safe people in your congregation:

Make small group ministries a centerpiece of congregational life. Moving people from the relative anonymity of sitting in the pews for worship to engaging others in a small group setting is probably the most significant thing a congregation can do to foster the development of strong interpersonal hospitality. Small groups foster the development of deep friendships, invite us to engage our faith journey more fully, encourage maturity in our spiritual journey, and provide what may be the best forum for caring for the needs of one another.

Teach the "one anothers." The New Testament is full of instruction in the form of "one another" statements, about how to live in right relationship with one another, or the practice of interpersonal hospitality. A listing of these is found in Appendix A of this volume. An excellent resource for small group study around this theme is Jim Van Yperen's *Authentic Community* curriculum based on the "one another" statements. (See suggested resources.)

Train the congregation in appropriate ways to deal with conflict. Conflict is an inevitable part of being in community. People will always have differing opinions and perspectives, their own agendas, and issues of control and power. How we deal with those is what makes Christian community unique. There are several resources to assist the local congregation in dealing with conflict in a biblical manner. I want to suggest two that I have found helpful:

- *Peacemaker Ministries*: provides a variety of small group training materials. This organization also trains persons in conflict coaching, mediation, and conflict resolution. (See suggested resources.)
- *Making Peace Ministry*: provides a variety of small group training materials and has trained coaches and mediators available to work with congregations in conflict situations. (See suggested resources.)

Provide training in caring for one another. Many congregations are training leaders, small group leaders, and pastoral care teams in the basic skills of caring for others in a variety of life situations. An excellent resource for this training is *Stephen Ministries,* which provides 50 hours of training to equip people to provide care to those experiencing difficult life situations. (See suggested resources.)

Build a congregational behavioral covenant. A behavioral covenant is an agreement built to clarify how members and leaders of a congregation will behave toward one another. It is a fairly common practice for leadership teams to develop a behavioral covenant for their work together, and it is becoming more common for congregations to follow this practice as well.

The key to a behavioral covenant is that it specifies the actual behaviors or ways that people will treat each other. For example: rather than saying "we will respect each other," the behavior might be "we will show respect for each other by listening to and seeking to understand the other person's point of view."

The behavioral covenant becomes the standard by which we do life together.

Questions for Leaders and Coaches Related to Interpersonal Hospitality:

- How are relationships encouraged and supported?
- What is the system for engaging participants in small groups or other discipleship partnering relationships (e.g. mentoring, coaching, spiritual friends)? What is the track record in the congregation for moving people from worship to connections with small groups or other forms of discipleship?
- What is the level of conflict within the congregation? What type of training is made available to encourage healthy conflict management?
- How do members of this congregation provide care for one another? How might they be encouraged to do so?
- What is the system for following up with regular worshipers who have been absent for two or more weeks?

INTENTIONAL HOSPITALITY

Refers to the practices of members and the congregation in making relational connections with people they don't know who are visiting and/or returning.

Intentional hospitality has two primary objectives: 1) to provide relational connections when newcomers join in worship and 2) to set an example for disciples in the way they might live beyond the church walls.

I attended a church a while back that has become very intentional about extending hospitality to those who come for the first time. When I arrived at the front door of the church I was welcomed by a greeter who shook my hand. Then an usher welcomed me and handed me a bulletin for worship. During the morning announcements welcome was extended by the pastor, and visitors were asked to stand, introduce themselves, and be welcomed by the congregation. An usher came and handed me a welcome packet with information about the congregation, a visitor information card, and a visitor nametag to wear. During the "greeting" time, several people shook my hand and said "welcome to worship." Following the worship service the pastor shook my hand as I exited the sanctuary. And, in the week following my visit to this church, I received a form letter from the pastor thanking me for visiting and expressing the hope that I would return.

My experience describes the more typical approaches of congregations in welcoming visitors or "guests," which is a term I prefer. To be perfectly blunt, these are what I call "platform level" practices. If they are missing (i.e..greeters or ushers, etc.) it is a red flag for guests. These things are expected as standard practice. Doing them doesn't make people feel welcome, but not doing them can make people feel unwelcome. Some of these standard practices actually work against us. For example, a vast majority of people has indicated that they would prefer not to be publicly recognized (read: are embarrassed) by having to stand and/or introduce themselves.

When people show up for the first time in worship, an overarching question is: "Do I fit in here?" or "Did people like me?"

There are a variety of factors at play in how people get the answer to that question. For example: in a congregation on the east coast of Florida, all the standard intentional hospitality expressions are in place (greeters, ushers, pastoral welcome), but this congregation goes beyond these "platform" expressions. Regular participants in the congregational life who have the gift of hospitality (hosts/hostesses) seek out newcomers and engage them in conversation, seeking to learn about them and their needs. If appropriate, they sit with the newcomer/family during worship. Following worship, these hosts/hostesses invite their new friends to join them at the hospitality center for refreshments and conversation. At the hospitality center the new friends are introduced to other regulars, appropriate staff, and the pastor. This expression of hospitality was already exceptional in our experience, and then they did something completely unexpected. The host/hostess invited their new friends to join them as their guests at a local restaurant for lunch and the opportunity to get to know them better!

As you might imagine, most people immediately felt like they fit in quite well.

I mentioned a hospitality center in the example above. It is one of the key ways that a church can support the making of connections. The hospitality center needs to be in a prominent location (not over in the fellowship hall) and have refreshments available for people as they gather to connect. Having people trained to invite newcomers to join them for some refreshments is important, as is having them introduce newcomers to other regular attenders, staff, and the pastor. It is also important to get the names of those who are guests so that follow-up may be accomplished.

In the previous example, the host/hostess invited guests to lunch to get to know them better. More common, but still exceptional, is the approach of taking a "welcome gift" (bread, pie, homemade jellies, etc.) to the home of a newcomer within 24 hours of their visit. This is a "cold call" visit just to drop off the gift and express a warm welcome. Doug Anderson, quoting Herb Miller, suggests: "be brief, be bright (positive), and be gone."[4] Opportunities to "sell" the church will come at another time. The timing of this visit is important. Waiting longer than 24 hours dramatically reduces the impact.

For follow-up visits to be accomplished, the church must have the name of those who visit. Getting this information can be accomplished in several ways: 1) have members write the name down as part of their conversation with newcomers, 2) have visitors complete a connect card or sign in on pew pads (this only works if members also complete this information), 3) review checks placed in the offering for names of those who are not regular attenders.

Another key for intentional hospitality is a connecting interview with newcomers. This is arranged after the second visit and is usually done by the pastor. The pastor should call to set up a time (45 minutes) to meet in the home of the newcomer. The purpose of the visit is to get to know them. This is a time to get accurate information about the family/individual (spelling of names, ages of children, schools attended, occupation, etc.). But even more important is the opportunity to discover how newcomers might be connected to existing small groups or to opportunities for service. The pastor does not make these connections ("sell" the church) but passes along information to group and ministry leaders. I cannot stress enough the importance of this "get to know you" session.

In a coaching call with a pastor serving a church about a year old, the pastor described a gathering of 40-50 for worship on a regular basis. But his description was of a congregation that changed every week. New people would come and might return weeks or months later, and some might never return.

If all the people who visited off-and-on were there on a more regular basis, the weekly worship attendance would be nearly double the current average.

What questions might you ask this pastor? Take a moment to note them below:

As I explored the regular practices with the pastor, it became clear that while a gift was delivered following worship (although typically 4–5 days later) and the guests were greeted by the pastor following worship, there was no real connection made with the congregation. There was also no "get to know you" type of conversation, so people had to figure out how to get connected on their own. In fact, the next step was a newcomers' (read: membership) class.

A tweaking of regular practices with an emphasis on the pastor making a real connection through an extended conversation immediately began to turn this situation around.

The end goal of hospitality is that people become disciples of Jesus and engaged in the life of the congregation. I recommend that this engagement take place at three points in the congregational life: worship, a small group or other accountable relationship, and some form of service.

The vital point here is that regular attenders of the congregation engage those who are newcomers in ways that make them feel really welcomed. Notice that I am saying "regular attenders" and not the pastor. It is meaningful when regular people make the effort to welcome others. Not so much for the pastor—he/she gets paid to do that! Some excellent resources are available for training your church in how to be a welcoming congregation through the ReThink Church materials. (See suggested resources.)

Questions for Leaders and Coaches Related to Intentional Hospitality:

- How does this congregation recognize visitors?
- What form of hospitality center does this congregation offer? Is there a place for people to gather and make connections? Are refreshments offered to facilitate this process? How is sensitivity to families with children demonstrated in the welcoming process?
- How does this congregation encourage regular participants to engage visitors? What form of training is provided? How is this monitored?
- What is the demographic mix of the congregation? How does this compare to the demographics of the surrounding community?
- What is the process for following up with first-time visitors? What is the role of the pastor?
- What is the system for connecting regular participants with first-time visitors to help them learn about congregational opportunities?
- Does this congregation offer an informational meeting to connect with visitors? Who has responsibility for this?
- What is the state of the congregation's facilities? Are they clean and inviting—especially the nursery and women's restroom?
- Is there adequate signage to assist newcomers?
- Describe the quality and variety of communication tools utilized by this congregation. Are they up-to-date? User-friendly? Do they avoid the use of "insider" and "churchy" language?

INVITATIONAL HOSPITALITY

Refers to the connections made by the congregation with people they don't know who are out in the community.

These connections usually take one of five forms. The following are brief descriptions of each:

Networking

This refers to the intentional building of relationships by the pastor and key lay leadership with those out in the community. I have seen over and over again the importance of these relationships forged with community leaders (Mayors, Police/Fire Chiefs, Home Owner Association Leaders, School Principals, etc.), local business owners, and social service organizations. I also recommend that pastors participate in the local Chamber of Commerce and organizations like Kiwanis and Rotary as ways to make connections.

This is important on three fronts: 1) the relationships forged will provide valuable insights into the workings of the community, 2) these relationships will provide further connections in the community, and 3) these relationships model for the congregation the kind of witness that each disciple can provide in their own circle of influence. Another benefit to these kinds of relationships is that through them the congregation will understand their own reputation within the community, which is important to know for future relationship-building and ministry opportunities.

A pastor I coach in the Northeast, following one of our coaching conversations, began to network and have conversations with some people he knew of who were influencers in the community. Not all were immediately receptive, but a conversation with one of them yielded so many additional contacts that the pastor was having trouble getting to all of them. This pastor has begun to encourage his core leadership to follow a similar pattern, and amazing connections are being made throughout the community.

Attractional Ministries

This refers to the types of events that serve to "attract" people to a congregation through providing visibility and interactions with the local community. Oftentimes these are identified as "outreach," but I believe this is a misnomer since most of them are done on church properties.

These events include things like Fall Festivals, Trunk 'R Treats (a Halloween gathering in the parking lot with candy distributed from decorated car trunks), Vacation Bible School, Pumpkin Patch, Christmas tree sales, block parties, concerts, yard sales, and the like. Sometimes these events get a bad rap and are discouraged. I don't feel like there is anything wrong with them—just that they are not a substitute for actually going out into the community. It's a "both-and" deal. The real value of any of these events (other than raising money) is that they are an opportunity for the building of relationships. By this I do not mean handing out church brochures. If the church is going to host an attractional event, there should be significant thought given to how the event could build contacts for the congregation (get names and addresses) and how the regular attenders will be encouraged to engage those who come from the community.

A word of caution is in order here: it is often the case that congregations get worn out and distracted doing event after event. The result is that they don't have the time or energy to actually go into the community and make a difference. I recommend that such activities be very limited (1–2 per year) to make space for more ministry of engagement.

My colleague Kim Shockley (a ministry coach and wife of a church planter/pastor) learned as part of a church planting team that it was essential to do these types of attractional ministries so that they could make the church name more visible in the community. One of the best opportunities was when they partnered with some stores during the late Christmas shopping season, setting up free gift-wrapping to wrap packages immediately after purchase. They had plenty of time to chat with the customers during the wrapping process and to invite them to attend the Christmas Eve services. Notice that this congregation moved away from the church grounds to do these "attractional" events.

Servant Evangelism

This concept was made popular by Steve Sjogren of the Vineyard Church. The basic model is that regular attenders of the congregation engage the local community through service projects. Steve describes servant evangelism as winning the heart before confronting the mind. In a great article, "94 Community Servant Evangelism Ideas for Your Church," he identifies some simple projects any congregation can engage. For example:

- Coffee Giveaways
- Bottled Water Giveaways
- Popcorn Giveaways
- Umbrella Escorts
- Trash Pick-Up
- Shoe Shines
- Surf Wax for surfers at the beach
- Clean Up at Food Courts
- Leaf Raking
- Tree Limb Trimming[5]

The opportunities for servant evangelism abound. It is an effective witness to God's love. One the most effective servant activities Kim's church experienced was taking boxes of donuts to fire stations, nursing homes, and other businesses where people had to work on Christmas Eve. The folks took the boxes with them to drop off on their way home from the worship services.

Ministries of Engagement

Often overlooked in the realm of hospitality is the impact of really making a difference in the community and inviting people to engage with the church. This is particularly true for our young adults, who often enter into a relationship with the church through service.

Ministries of engagement will be discussed further in the chapter on Service. For now, let's just say that they are long-term, sacrificial, and needs-focused acts of service to the community. Sometimes the people being served by these impactful ministries will be drawn to the congregational life. Sometimes people with a heart for making a difference will be drawn to the service being offered and then to the community offering it. Sometimes both will happen.

Marketing

This is discussed last because it is the least effective of all the invitational hospitality concepts presented here.

Typical approaches include newspaper advertisements, yellow book advertisements, direct mailing, telephone soliciting, and electronic media, including the website.

As a general rule, newspaper and phone book advertisements are relatively ineffective. Direct mail yields results in the range of one response for every 200 mailers or about ½ of 1% and is fairly expensive. Telephone soliciting is usually seen as an annoyance today.

The website of the church is today's equivalent of an advertisement in the yellow pages a decade or two ago. It is a "must do" and "must do well." Websites must be easy to navigate, invitational, and full of pictures, stories, and white space.

Current research indicates that as many as 90% of people will visit a church's website before making a decision to attend. That's huge! If the website is going to be such a primary tool for extending hospitality, it is important that the site represent the church well. The following are some suggestions about providing a welcoming site:

- Invest the resources to create a professional-looking site. The quality of your website is considered a reflection of the excellence with which you do ministry.

- Keep the website current. I worked with a church a couple of years ago that had a pastor's message from the previous pastor who had moved two years earlier.

- Have worship times clearly identified with a description of the style of worship included.

- Provide clear directions to your church location. Many websites now include a link to Google Directions.

- Provide information about childcare; without this you may lose young families.

- Include information about your staff. The best sites even include a personal statement from staff members.

- Include a place to listen to current messages from worship services.

- Share stories about lives that are changed and the difference the church is making in the community.

Many sites I have visited actually include an itinerary for newcomers through the website. Information is provided about attire for the service selected, availability and location of childcare, and a time frame for activities the newcomer could experience.

Questions for Leaders and Coaches Related to Invitational Hospitality:

- What kind of networking (building of relationships) takes place by the leadership of this congregation out in the community?
- What types of activities are provided to engage the community and promote visibility?
- What types of services are offered through the church to support the needs of those living in the community?
- How is this congregation involved in direct service to the community?
- How are regular participants in the congregation equipped to share their faith and engage those beyond the church?
- How does this congregation support community events?
- How does the congregation see participation in the life of the community as a ministry of the congregation?
- What types of marketing tools are employed by this congregation?
- How does the church website reflect a posture of hospitality?

INCARNATIONAL HOSPITALITY

Refers to the personal engagement by regular participants in the congregation in building relationships with those we know outside the church in order to be Christ to the unchurched.

People come to a relationship with Jesus through a relationship with other people. I hope this doesn't come as a surprise to you.

Some people are drawn to a relationship with Jesus through the witness of our lives—how we treat others, the honest way we do business, the priorities we live by, the giving of ourselves to others. They may seek to get to know us and discover how those dimensions of our lives have been developed.

More commonly we are the ones building relationships with those outside the church in order to be Christ in their lives. The scope of possibilities for this is almost endless. One new church pastor I know began her congregation by building relationships with young mothers as they had play time at the parks and "mom" time in each others' homes. The relationships she fostered developed into friendships and ultimately into relationships with Jesus. It is the perfect witness to the Emmaus Walk (a spiritual formation retreat sponsored by the Upper Room, General Board of Discipleship) teaching: *Make a Friend, Be a Friend, Bring a Friend to Christ.*[6]

Christians believe that life finds its meaning in a relationship with Jesus. Since that is true, it becomes the responsibility of every disciple to not only be in that relationship, but to help others discover the relationship as well.

Congregations that do incarnational hospitality well help their members discover ways to connect with people in times when they are most open to an expression of God's love for them. For example, people going through major life transitions are often open to support (e.g. marriage, birth of a child, moving to a new community or a new job). People who are going through crises in life (divorce, grief, loss of property, aging, health issues, etc.) also tend to be open to the loving support offered by disciples.

The key to incarnational hospitality is that we are building relationships beyond the walls of the church. However, in my work with churches around the country, I have found focus in this area to be lacking; in fact, just the opposite is generally true. The longer people are involved in the church, the fewer people they are in relationship with outside the church... by a long shot!

Alan Hirsch, in his book *The Forgotten Ways,* provides one of the best descriptions of incarnational hospitality I have come across:

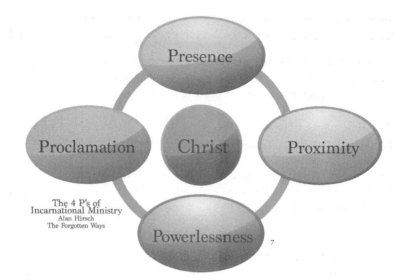

The 4 P's of
Incarnational Ministry
Alan Hirsch
The Forgotten Ways

Presence refers to the act of actually being with people. It is what Jesus did when he came into our world. As noted in John 1:14, "The Word became flesh and blood, and moved into the neighborhood" (The Message). Henri Nouwen, in his focus on hospitality, notes:

> "It is a privilege to have the time to practice this simple ministry of presence. Still, it is not as simple as it seems...I wonder more and more if the first thing shouldn't be to know people by name, to eat and drink with them, to listen to their stories and tell your own, and to let them know...that you do not simply like them—but truly love them."[8]

Proximity refers to becoming meaningfully involved in the lives of those being served. There is a significant shift that takes place between the ideas of presence and proximity. In the former, we are close and involved enough to be in a casual relationship; in the latter, we are engaged in ways that make a difference in people's lives.

For example, in the second congregation I served, we offered a meal each week for the homeless, lonely, and hungry in the community. At first the focus was on getting people (including leadership) involved in preparing, serving, setting up, and cleaning up. We greeted people and got to know many by name. We were practicing the ministry of presence.

A decision was made that some of the volunteers would not be involved in cooking and serving the meal, but would actually eat the meal that was being served and sit with the people the meal was designed to be in ministry to. This immediately opened the door to significant relationships, a deeper understanding of needs, and more opportunities to be in service. That was a ministry of proximity.

Powerlessness refers to the understanding that we are servants. Way too often we approach our ministries from a position of power ("fix," "help," "change"). The powerlessness dimension of incarnational hospitality focuses on the servant nature of Christ through us that empowers others.

Proclamation of course refers to the ability and willingness to share the gospel message. As Peter put it: "Always be prepared to give an answer to everyone who asks you to give the reason for the hope that you have. But do this with gentleness and respect" (1 Peter 3:15).

Proclamation comes last for a reason.

People are most open to the gospel message when we have built a relationship with them, when they know we care about them, and when they understand that we are most concerned with empowering them rather than having power over them. Then we can share, with integrity, the Good News of Jesus Christ.

Since we also understand that people are encouraged in their faith journeys as they are nurtured in Christian community, these relationships formed outside of the church become the bridge to engaging people in the larger community of faith.

It's no secret. Most churches (somewhere around 80%) are plateaued or in decline when it comes to participation in worship. Leadership teams all across the country sit and bemoan the fact that fewer people, and certainly fewer younger people and fewer non-Christian people, are coming to church. They often ask, "What can we do to turn this around?"

My first question is, "Who have you asked to come to church with you in the last month?" For some reason leadership teams are often surprised by the question. It never occurred to them that this is a responsibility of *every disciple.*

Current research indicates that for those who are unchurched, somewhere between 60–80% responded that they would come to church if someone invited them.

However, the church has a role in supporting the regular attenders in inviting their friends, relatives, associates (work), and neighbors. Some churches provide members with business cards that include the worship times and directions to the church. Many churches provide postcards with information about a new sermon series or seasonal focus that regular attenders can use to invite friends.

Doug Anderson, in his book *The Race to Reach Out,* shares a seasonal focus approach used by Joe Harding:

- A few weeks before the invitational focus of the season, 3x5 cards are distributed to the congregation.
- Each participant is asked to write down the names of 5 people they would like to see come to worship.
- Participants are encouraged to take the cards home and display them in a prominent place where they would be reminded to pray daily for the people named on the cards.
- A couple of weeks prior to the invitational focus event, participants are encouraged to extend an invitation.
- In worship the participants are asked to, by a show of hands, be accountable for praying for and making the invitation.

The result was an increase of 50% on these invitational Sundays and a congregation that experienced significant long-term growth.[9]

The key to personal invitations is that they are personal—face-to-face if possible—and focused on "come with" rather than "come sometime."

Questions for Leaders and Coaches Related to Incarnational Hospitality:

- How are people encouraged and supported in the building of relationships beyond the church?
- How are these relationships recognized and celebrated by the pastor and/or congregation?
- What types of personal acts of service/mission are being performed by regular participants of this congregation?
- How does this congregation use the connecting points of servant evangelism, needs-based evangelism, and ministries of engagement to build relationships in the community and invite participation in congregational life?

Diagnosing the Level of Hospitality

In addition to the coaching questions presented for the dimensions of hospitality, there are a variety of tools that the coach may find helpful. The following is a brief description of a sampling of these tools and where one might find more information:

Professions of Faith: The goal of hospitality is to pave the way for those outside of the church to discover the love of God through a relationship with Jesus Christ. A standard measure of the effectiveness of our hospitality is the trend of the congregation in the area of professions of faith. This information is readily available in most congregations.

Communication Tools: The website, church newsletters, bulletins, and other printed materials utilized by the congregation can provide great insight into the culture of hospitality for a congregation.

For example, the website is often the first venue of hospitality experienced by those seeking a church. Does the church have a website? Is it easily navigated? Is it current? Is there information about locating the church and service times and attire?

Or, consider the bulletin. One church I worked with had a big negative statement about the use of cell phones in worship right at the top of the worship bulletin. That's probably not the first thing you want people to see! As a general rule, churches should avoid negative signage in any form (e.g. keep off the grass, no drinks in the Sanctuary, etc.). Churches also use a lot of "churchy" language with the expectation that everyone knows what it means. If you are going to use the Gloria Patri, print or project the text! If you are going to use the Lord's Prayer, print or project the version you use so there is no confusion about "trespasses" or "sins."

Readiness 360: This unique online survey (www.readiness360.org) measures the spiritual intensity, missional alignment, dynamic relationships, and cultural openness of your congregation. Designed to serve as an indicator for readiness to multiply, this is a great resource for measuring church health.[10]

Mystery Visitors: It is easy and inexpensive to have someone from outside the church visit the normal worship experience and then report on how they were welcomed and engaged. Excellence in Ministry Coaching has a simple report form that is available at no cost (www.emc3coaching.com).[11]

Welcoming Congregation Certification: United Methodist Communications provides an assessment and training for becoming certified "welcoming congregations." We recommend participation in this training.[12]

Real Discipleship Survey: This tool is designed for both individual use and as a congregational survey. It highlights the maturity level of individuals in several areas of the discipleship journey, including Hospitality. This tool is available from www.emc3coaching.com. For congregational use, the survey is taken by a representative group and then averaged in each of the dimensions of discipleship as an indicator of the level of maturity for the congregation as a whole.[13]

Congregational Survey: The measurement of hospitality practices as perceived by the congregation is part of a more comprehensive survey of congregational health. This is offered as both a pdf download and in a Survey Monkey format which gives an analysis (www.emc3coaching.com).[14]

Discovering the Possibilities: This facilitated congregational workshop includes a variety of insights into the culture of hospitality extended by a congregation through congregational interview, discussion about missional vital signs, facility review, and the Real Discipleship Survey.[15]

Leadership Team Assessment: This document (available from www.emc3coaching.com) is a set of questions for local church leadership teams to consider. The practices of hospitality, worship, discipleship, service, and generosity are all included.[16]

Most of these and other tools are available in *Tips, Tools, and Activities for Coaching Church Leaders,* our companion resource for *Shift.* (See www.emc3coaching.com.)

Getting Started: Platform Stuff

In my work with congregations across the country, I have found several practices that are essential to the development of a culture of congregational hospitality. These do not represent the end-goal of hospitality. Instead, these are the foundations upon which a culture of hospitality is built. I call them *Platform Stuff.* In and of themselves they do not produce a culture of hospitality. These are the things that people expect to be in place. If you don't have them, people will notice and likely determine that this congregation doesn't really care about welcoming newcomers. Once these are in place it is possible to develop the practices that create a culture of hospitality.

Clean and Inviting Facilities

It is common practice for most families to clean up their homes (do the dishes, vacuum the floors, pick up the toys, etc.) when they are expecting guests. I suggest that the same should be true for the family of God as we prepare for guests. The cleanliness of our facilities is a statement about the value we place on guests and the excellence with which we do life together.

The problem is that we who regularly attend worship become so accustomed to things (items collecting in the corner of a hallway, dingy and worn carpets, used bulletins left in the pew racks, peeling paint in the worship center, etc.) that there is a lack of awareness about the way newcomers see these.

It might be helpful to have someone from outside your church walk the facilities with your trustees to point out areas for improvement.

The cleanliness of facilities and quality of landscaping will not attract people to your church as a general rule. However, the lack of it might keep them away.

Attractive and Safe Nursery

At the top of the list for most churches is having more young families as part of the congregation. At the top of the list for young families is having excellent nursery care. It is critical that these facilities are both attractive and safe.

Young moms, who carefully select a daycare center for their children, will be less than enthusiastic about dropping off the same child to a 15-year-old sitting in a rocking chair while several infants crawl around on a dingy area rug.

Are the facilities clean? Are they well-stocked with toys that are sanitized regularly? Is there some form of training/certification required for nursery workers? Is there an identification system with care instructions for each child? Is there a system for contacting parents in worship should the need arise? Is the nursery located in close proximity to the worship space?

Welcome and Hospitality Center

Every worshiping congregation should have a welcome and hospitality center. This is a clearly identified space where knowledgeable guides are present to help newcomers find their way around the campus, escort parents and children to the appropriate classrooms, help people locate the restrooms, etc.

The welcome center is also a centralized place where guests can get printed information about the ministries of the congregation. Some congregations use this center as the distribution point for gifts prepared for guests in worship.

It is my belief that this space should also provide a place for people to connect and begin the process of building relationships. Having coffee, juice, and healthy snacks is a good start; having people from the congregation who invite newcomers to join them for refreshments is even better.

It is often a surprise to congregations that having refreshments located in the fellowship hall or a classroom doesn't seem to be very effective in reaching guests. If this really is a hospitality center, it needs to be clearly visible, central, and identified so that people unfamiliar with the campus will make this point of contact.

This space is all about relationship building, which is what hospitality is all about.

Training the Congregation

The importance of having people from the congregation connect with guests and start the process of building relationships cannot be overemphasized. This, unfortunately, is not the natural way for people to do church; they need to be trained. The Rethink Church materials make a couple of excellent suggestions for this training:

- 3-minute rule: For three minutes following the close of the worship service, ask regular participants to make a point of engaging in conversation with guests and people they do not know rather than rushing out or talking just with friends. It takes about three minutes for a guest to exit following the worship experience, and this provides a forum for engaging them relationally.

- 10-foot rule: Ask all worship participants to make a point of entering into conversation with everyone within a 10 foot radius of where they are sitting at some point prior to or following worship.[17]

Encourage the conversations described to focus on getting to know what the guest is seeking and how the church might be helpful. Help guests to connect with others from the congregation, particularly the pastor or staff member who might be of assistance to help him/her to make a connection. Gathering at a hospitality center around refreshments is a good way to facilitate this.

Greetings During Worship

As a general rule, recent studies have indicated that guests in worship prefer not to be asked to stand and identify themselves (or sit while everyone else stands!). They prefer some anonymity or at least the choice to put themselves out there. This is particularly true of those younger than retirement age.

Having said that, there are exceptions to the rule. For those congregations with a large demographic of seasonal participants it is often widely accepted to share who you are and where you are from. This provides a natural connection between the guest and regular participants from the same area of the country and often initiates the building of relationships.

The most effective greeting is not from the pulpit but from regular people sitting close by who make a point of entering into a conversation. These connections can then be used to get guests to a welcome center where they can find information about the church or be "mugged" (gift of a church mug or other small token).

Informational Meetings

It is my recommendation that every congregation have regular (monthly at least) informational meetings where guests can learn about the focus of that particular church, opportunities to grow as disciples, and opportunities to engage the local community. This is a great time to get to know the heart of the pastor and the congregation.

Not every church will be a good fit for every person. The informational meetings provide an opportunity for guests to figure out if this is the right place for them. It is also a great way to continue building relationships.

Please note: this is not intended to be a new member class. It is not the place to review the history of the denomination or local church. It's all about connections!

Professional-Quality Communications

A consideration too often overlooked as impacting hospitality is the quality of our communications. The website for a church is often the first place that people go to begin forming an impression of your congregation. Is the website attractive? Easily negotiated? Current? Helpful?

Is the signage for your facilities adequate to assist people in finding classrooms? Worship center? Restrooms? Is there negative signage: "Don't do this? Don't enter here? Don't walk here?"

Are your bulletins and newsletter attractive, with plenty of "white space," illustrations, and of course, useful information presented with good grammar and spelling?

If a PowerPoint is used in worship, is it attractive, checked for grammar and spelling, and not overloaded with too much content? Is there an operator who is trained and experienced to make sure that slides and videos are in place on cue?

Guest Follow-Up

An important part of hospitality is the follow-up done with guests in your worship services. At minimum, there should be a letter from the pastor (handwritten is best) welcoming them and expressing appreciation for their participation. A more personal call from someone in the congregation is a plus.

Some congregations provide a brief visit (not necessarily even going into the home) to deliver fresh-baked goods or jellies (preferably made by someone in the congregation) and share a welcome. This provides a "personal connect" without being overwhelmed.

A Behavioral Covenant

Finally, back to where we began our discussion around the theme of hospitality. The manner in which people within the congregation treat each other is a significant factor in the level of comfort experienced by guests.

I have found it helpful for congregations to enter into a Behavioral Covenant—a document developed by the congregation that clearly delineates how participants will interact. This document is written around specific behaviors that all agree to engage. This goes a long way toward building positive interpersonal hospitality.

A PowerPoint presentation and script designed to walk a congregational leadership team through the process of developing a behavioral covenant is available through www.emc3coaching.com.[18]

Suggested Resources for Coaches and Congregations Related to Hospitality:

- *The Race to Reach Out: Connecting Newcomers to Christ in a New Century,* Douglas T. Anderson and Michael J. Coyner, Abingdon Press, 2004.

- *Right Here, Right Now: Everyday Mission for Everyday People,* Alan Hirsch and Lance Ford, Baker Books, 2011.

- *Reaching Out: The Three Movements of the Spiritual Life,* Henri J. M. Nouwen, Image Books, 1975.

- *The Inviting Church: a study of new member assimilation,* Roy M. Oswald and Speed B. Leas, Alban Institute, 1987.

- *50 Ways to Build Strength to Welcome New People,* Lewis Center for Church Leadership, www.churchleadership.com.

- *Unbinding the Gospel: Real Life Evangelism,* Martha Grace Reese, Chalice Press, 2008.

- *Peacemaker Ministries,* www.peacemaker.net

- *Making Peace: A Guide to Overcoming Church Conflict,* Jim Van Yperen, Moody Publishers, 2002.

- *Catch: A Churchwide Program for Invitational Evangelism,* Debi Nixon with Adam Hamilton, Abingdon Press, 2012.

- *United Methodist Welcoming Congregation Certification,* United Methodist Communications, www.UMCom.org/site/c.mrLZJ9PFKmG/b.6375629/k.B30E/Welcoming_Certified_Churches.htm.

- *Authentic Community: Practicing the one another commands,* Jim Van Yperen, ChurchSmart Resources, 2008.

- *Stephen Ministries,* www.stephenministries.org.

- *Get Their Name: Grow Your Church by Building New Relationships,* by Bob Farr, Doug Anderson, and Kay Kotan, Abingdon Press, 2013.

shift 2:

From Worship as an Event to Worship as a Lifestyle

*"So here's what I want you to do, God helping you: Take your everyday,
ordinary life—your sleeping, eating, going-to-work, and
walking-around life—and place it before God as an offering."*
The Apostle Paul, Romans 12:1 (The Message)

*"You are and always will be a worshiper. It's what you do. You can't
help it. You can't stop it. You can't live without it. But you can choose
where you invest it... We're created to worship."*
Louie Giglio, *The Air I Breathe*[1]

It was Saturday evening in the middle of an amazing spiritual retreat
weekend. The community had gathered for worship out in the country in a
white-framed church that had to be a century old. In this space where the
saints had sung praises and prayed prayers and shared the Word of God
together, the Spirit was palpable. We joined the communion of the saints in
worship as we lifted our voices in praise and prayer, reflected on the Scriptures together, shared our stories, recommitted our lives, and celebrated at
the table of the Feast.

In preparation for the arrival of participants for worship, we lit our
candles in the darkened space and sang praise to God who had been at work
in such amazing ways. As they, with glowing faces, processed down the
aisles between pews, there was not a dry eye in the room. We were there to
celebrate what God had been doing. We were there to witness to our faith.
And we were there to encourage the faith of others.

As we left that holy space, each of us understood that our lives had
been altered in some unmistakable way. We were no longer on our own. We

were part of something bigger than ourselves. We were passionate participants in the mission of God.

There was really nothing especially unique about the elements of the
worship service. They were much the same as most worship services in
which I have participated. But there was something unique about the experience of this particular worship event. In fact, it was so powerful that in
over 25 years of ministry I have had a passion, a longing if you will, to be
part of making this kind of impact on people's lives week after week as they
too gather for worship.

As I reflected on the experience I had some insights that have helped
me form weekly worship experiences and participate in impacting lives for
over two decades. For example:

- It wasn't about us. The worship experience was about God and focusing our praise and thanksgiving toward the source of our being.
- It wasn't showy. The experience had been carefully planned and was
  well-conducted, but we were careful to be open to what the Spirit
  wanted to do.
- It was focused. The preaching/teaching of the Word was practical
  and focused on putting into practice what God wanted for our lives.
- It was experiential. The participants in worship were engaged in acts
  of worship rather than spectators in a worship event.
- It was relational. We found a joy in gathering with other believers
  having a similar focus in life and were encouraged as we encouraged
  others.

I'd like to say that this has been the norm for all the worship I have participated in over the years and the experience of those in worship together
in many diverse places. However, my experience has been that this is not
always the case.

Observations about Worship

Let's consider some observations about worship from current research and
from my experiences with transforming congregations:

- Worship is not just about an event. It is a lifestyle. What we do in
  corporate worship has the opportunity to equip people to be better
  worshipers the rest of the week.
- A very small percentage of participants in worship report that they

have experienced the presence of God during corporate worship over the past year.

- We are designed to worship. The question is what will be the focus of our worship?

- Worship includes both the offering of our lips (praises) and the sacrifices of our lives (service).

- There is no "right" worship style. What is "right" is that the congregation finds a way to connect with the community it is called to serve.

- Worship is the centerpiece of a Christian community. The excellence and effectiveness with which we offer worship has significant impact on every other dimension of ministry (discipleship, hospitality, service, and generosity).

- Worship experiences that are the result of team planning and execution tend to be more creative and engaging.

A Theology of Worship

Worship is about giving honor and glory to God. At a corporate level, worship is the gathering of the community of faith to praise God, learn the ways of God, and be challenged to take the next steps in our commitment as disciples. At a personal level, worship is about living life in a way that honors God in all that we are and do. There is great value to the corporate worship experience. Yet, at the heart of worship, as songwriter Matt Redman puts it, is a life where every single breath is God's—where it's all about Jesus.

> *King of endless worth*
> *No one could express*
> *How much You deserve*
> *Though I'm weak and poor*
> *All I have is Yours*
> *Every single breath*
>
> *I'll bring You more than a song*
> *For a song in itself*
> *Is not what You have required*
> *You search much deeper within*
> *Through the way things appear*
> *You're looking into my heart*

I'm coming back to the heart of worship
And it's all about You
It's all about You, Jesus
I'm sorry, Lord, for the thing I've made it
When it's all about You
It's all about You, Jesus[2]

Great worship prepares worshipers to live this kind of worshipful life. It moves us from worship as an event to worship as a lifestyle.

For example:

- How I choose to use my time
- How I choose to use the resources God has provided
- The focus I place on loving my wife and family
- The way I interact with a difficult person
- The priority I place on spending time with God
- My faithfulness in following through on commitments
- The excellence with which I perform the tasks of my job

These, of course, just begin to scratch the surface; thus the Shift from worship as an event to worship as a lifestyle.

Corporate worship and worship as a lifestyle go hand in hand. Corporate worship prepares us to worship as a lifestyle and when we practice worship as a lifestyle it strengthens the celebration of corporate worship.

A LITURGICAL FLOW OF WORSHIP

If the goal of worship is both to provide an opportunity to be engaged in the presence of God and to equip participants to develop a lifestyle of worship, how might one coach the congregation in this area of its ministry? Since many churches use the traditional liturgical flow of a corporate worship experience, let's start there.

Gathering ⇨ Praise & Prayer ⇨ Proclamation ⇨
Response to the Word ⇨ Sending Forth

Gathering

This refers to the coming together of the people of God to engage in prayer, praise, learning the ways of God, and taking next steps in the journey of discipleship. In the gathering, people are either led to greater engagement and anticipation for what is to come or they are left feeling like an outsider and begin to disengage from the worship service. All of this happens before the preacher begins the message! A couple of quick and easy measurements help you get a sense of the effectiveness of the "gathering": is there a stagnancy in the worship participation with few new people showing up OR lots of new people floating through and few sticking around? Either is an indication that something is wrong.

I once served a congregation in a small town surrounded by several retirement communities. A regular worship participant from one of these communities shared how a group from her area became involved in the church. She said, "We sat outside in our car and watched people coming out of worship. When we saw that they were smiling and happy to be there, we knew it was the right place for us!"

Praise and Prayer

In some congregations this is actually considered the "worship" part of the service and the proclamation the "teaching" part. I don't like this distinction. However, the praise and prayer component of the worship service is the beginning of a focus on the God we have come to worship. It is an opportunity to set the stage for the message to be proclaimed. As such, it is important that the musical selections and the prayers voiced relate to and support the main theme of the worship experience.

Proclamation

The "proclamation" of the Word is usually considered the reading of the Scripture lesson and the message proclaimed from that lesson. This is certainly the core of proclamation. But there is much more! In the contemporary church, we tend to get stuck on the idea of the centrality of the message proclaimed. In my first appointment, the pulpit stood 6 feet high, was made of granite and shaped like a double-edged sword, with a 1–2 square foot area for standing to preach. It was placed in front of the altar and the baptismal font, blocking the view except from each extreme side. There was even a brochure explaining the placement and design of the pulpit emphasizing the "centrality of preaching" in the worship experience. You can imagine the reaction when the new senior pastor and I moved the pulpit to the side of the chancel and preached at floor level walking around!

The proclamation of the Word can be made in a variety of ways. For example, there are several websites that offer short video presentations related to a broad spectrum of themes. A drama team might prepare a 3–5 minute skit to proclaim or introduce a worship theme. A dramatic reading of the Scriptures might be prepared. There might be some type of interactive activity to have the congregation engage with the theme. The point here is that the worship design team should seek the most effective and creative way possible to help make the point and make it stick.

This may also be a good place to introduce a very important concept. To use the words of Cathy Townley (worship coach and author), "Right now, in many of our churches, worship is not our focus. The worship *service* is....I learned that worship is our relationship with God. That means worship is our way of life. Worship changes our lives. If our lives don't change... we are not worshiping."[3]

I agree. Worship is not about an event. It is about a lifestyle. One of the roles of the worship event is to better prepare the congregation to worship as a lifestyle. This certainly includes the presentation of messages that are relevant to people's lives and giving people an opportunity to respond to what God is speaking into their lives during the worship event.

It also includes the introduction of spiritual disciplines. It came as no surprise when my friend Kim Shockley shared that the "Toward Vitality" research project (a United Methodist denominational research project) showed that a congregation that actively participates in the spiritual disciplines of prayer, meditation, Bible study, and other activities that draw us closer to God is more vital because their corporate relationship with God spills over onto others! As she writes in the final report on the project describing congregations experiencing transformation: "Worship was a source of discipleship formation....Most churches mentioned the practice of John Wesley's means of grace: works of mercy, worship, Bible study, prayer, and even fasting."[4]

While these very things serve as catalysts for maturity as disciples of Jesus Christ, the vast majority of our congregations simply will not attend a class on prayer or spiritual disciplines. During my pastoral ministry I regularly offered classes on prayer. Much to my surprise (a little sarcasm), only about 1–2% of the congregation participated, and they were already the prayer "warriors" of the congregation!

So, to take advantage of the largest opportunity to help people develop their spiritual lives—the worship service—we began to introduce the practice of spiritual disciplines and methods of prayer into the structure of the worship service. These added a new element of creativity to the worship experience and introduced the congregation to tools that would serve them well as they developed their personal worship journey.

Response to the Word

Communion

I am a huge proponent of including Communion as part of every regular worship experience. In the context of the last local congregation I served, this was our practice in every style of worship we offered. There is something about the action of physically receiving the elements of communion and spending time in prayer at the communion rail that allowed God the opportunity to speak into people's lives in that moment.

We also provided prayer partners who were available during the communion time to pray with those seeking intercessory support and those making commitments or recommitments of their lives to living as fully devoted disciples. These prayer partners also provided anointing with oil as a vessel of God's healing grace.

In addition to the regular practice of communion, every worship experience included prayer altars located around the sanctuary. These were simple stations that included a tray with sand and a large candle (already lit). Also provided were white birthday cake–style candles that congregants could light from the candle in the center and place in the tray with sand while they offered a prayer of intercession or petition. It was usually the case that people would be lined up waiting for an opportunity to practice this act of prayer.

There is something very significant about physically engaging people in response to the proclamation of the Word.

We would also regularly seek other ways to engage people in response to the message. For example, when speaking about the baptism of Jesus, we followed by offering people the opportunity, as they came for communion, to renew their baptismal vows. When preaching about the woman caught in adultery, each congregant was invited to take a small pebble from a bowl beside the communion rail and carry it in their pocket for the week as a reminder about "casting the first stone." On Thanksgiving we created a "wall of thanksgiving" (our version of the wailing wall) on which people could write prayers of thanksgiving. One Easter, working with a theme of the death of Jesus "bridging the gap" between our sinfulness and God's holiness, we built a bridge that people were invited to walk across on their way to communion.

You get the idea. Creatively engaging people in response to the Word makes for a memorable and powerful experience.

Offering

Oftentimes the offering component of the worship service is treated as "dead space" to fill with an anthem or other musical offering. It has been my experience that there is a great disconnect between the giving of our tithes and offerings and our ability to see that these gifts are making a kingdom difference. People just don't seem to connect the dots. And if they can't see the difference their offerings are making (other than paying the bills, which doesn't seem to get people excited) people are less generous. The offering is a great time to introduce the congregation to the impact of ministries, the witness of transformed lives because of the ministries of the church, and the amazing ways the kingdom work is done globally through the connectional system.

Personal testimonies, video testimonies, and prepared video presentations from www.UMCom.org are just a few of the many ways the offering time in the worship experience can be used as a tool to encourage generosity.[5]

This is also a time to witness that the offering is not just about our money. Celebrate the offerings people are making with their lives and their time to make a difference in the community.

If all this is correct and the offering time in worship is not just a way to collect money to pay the budget, it calls into question a significant trend I am finding in some parts of the country. The offering is treated as something we are embarrassed about or something we downplay as almost unnecessary. Offering receptacles are placed at the back of the worship space and people can make a contribution if they think about it. Sometimes the opportunity to make an offering is not even mentioned in the worship service.

People need to be encouraged and taught to be generous. It is part of our spiritual growth.

Sending Forth

This is far more than just the "concluding remarks" of the worship event. The sending forth is an opportunity to challenge the congregation to take the next step in the spiritual journey, to do something specific in the following week based on what God has been doing through the worship event, and to proclaim God's blessing and power to live as the people God has called us to be.

Since one of the things we hope to accomplish as we send people forth is the building of relationships and the expression of hospitality, this is also a great opportunity to encourage this practice. Our invitation to this practice went something like this: "Our hospitality center is located just outside the worship center, and there are lots of great refreshments for you to enjoy. If you are sitting close to someone you do not know, invite them to join you for a cup of coffee or juice and take an opportunity to begin a new friendship."

This invitation took the pressure off "locating visitors" and visitors wondering if someone would choose them (imagine choosing teams in elementary school and the fear that created). Everyone was encouraged to engage someone else in building a relationship.

Questions for Leaders and Coaches Related to a Liturgical Flow of Worship:

- Who is the target group for the worship experience? How does this form the way worship is designed?
- What is the "mood" of the gathered worship community? What are their facial expressions and body language? How do the choir and those leading worship reflect a worshiping attitude?
- What is the quality of printed materials distributed for worship? How are the materials designed to reflect an expectation that those unfamiliar with your worship experience might be present?
- How is the worship experience designed to reflect a culture of excellence?
- How does the leadership of worship include all ages and demographic groups represented in the congregation? Are there ages or groups missing?
- What is the musical style most prevalent in your worship experience? Does this reflect the demographics of the congregation? Of the community?
- What opportunities exist in your worship for participants to take a next step in their discipleship journey?
- How are people invited to explore a relationship with this community of faith?

WORSHIP THAT CONNECTS

The liturgical flow described previously is a fairly standard approach to designing worship. It has been used in pretty much the same form for centuries. Yet, when regular churchgoers were surveyed by George Barna, a significant number admitted that they haven't experienced God's presence in the past year. In other words, the experience didn't connect. As Barna writes: "Our studies show that 14 percent of adult believers admit that they have never experienced the presence of God, 14 percent have experienced His presence but not in the past year, and 72 percent have encountered God in a real way within the past year. In a typical worship service, about half claim that they did not experience God's presence or feel that they interacted with Him in a personal way."[6]

I believe that one of the reasons for the disconnect may be our lack of central theme or message, connecting the individual parts to the whole worship experience. For example, we may sing about the majesty of God, pray for the sick in our midst, hear a message about the lost sheep, and are then sent out to be lights in the world. It's hard to imagine how this experience would be transforming or inspire us to develop a lifestyle of worship.

Another reason that people may not connect with the worship experience is that we who design it give little consideration to the ways in which people receive, process, and act on the information and experience. A planning tool that I have found helpful (in both worship and curriculum design) is a resource called 4MAT. This tool, created by Dr. Bernice McCarthy, founder of About Learning, Inc., considers the various learning styles (closely associated with the MBTI for those familiar with this tool) and helps in engaging all learners when creating a learning experience.[7]

Let's start with how learners learn:

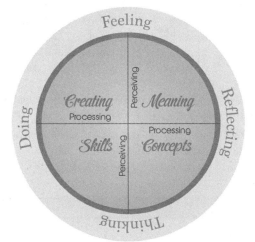

Notice the two axes of this diagram. The vertical axis or line refers to how learners *perceive*, in other words, how they take in the things they learn.

Some people sense or feel things; others have to think about the things they learn. The horizontal axis or line refers to how learners *process* or what they do with what they take in. Some people process what they take in by reflecting on it, mulling it over. Others process by doing something with what they take in.

Now let's look at how these differences in how people perceive and process produce different types of learners:

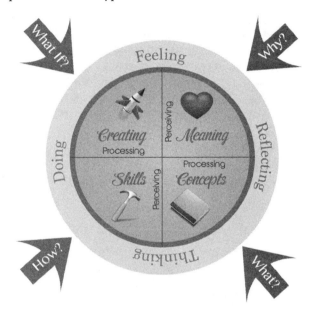

Each learning style can be identified by a question:

- Why?—These worshipers feel and then reflect. They have to know why something is significant and sense it in their hearts before they will engage with it. They might be described as "heart" people because they need to feel deeply to connect.

- What?—These worshipers think and then reflect. They need information before they can begin to process what is being asked of them. They might be described as "book" people, because they need content or concepts to connect.

- How?—These worshipers think and then do. Like the "what" people, they need information, but they process by putting what they learn into action. They might be described as "tool" people, because they need *practical* content to connect. If these worshipers can't do something with what they have learned, the learning is lost.

- What If?—These worshipers feel and then do. Once they sense something is important, they are already moving to doing and applying what they are taking in to other parts of their lives. They might be described as "rocket" people, because once they feel deeply, they are ready to take off.

In every worshiping community all four types are represented. If we fail to address any one of the questions, people will leave without actually engaging with the Word in any significant way.

An example of worship designed around the 4MAT Wheel:

From the example above you might imagine the following connecting points: the imagery of crowns displayed on the altar table along with music celebrating Jesus as King begins to connect with the 'why' as the congregation begins to explore the idea of Jesus being King in their lives. The message provides the content (the 'what') for people to begin reflecting on what it would mean for Jesus to actually rule their lives. The witness of how someone else is living out (the "how") and the invitation to take the next step helps people see how it might be possible for Jesus to rule their lives. And, the challenge to begin the day in an act of submission and dependence on the King provides the "what if" real life response to the Word proclaimed.

We have long heard it said that people remember less than 10% of what they hear from our worship messages. But what people take away from the worship experience is based on more than what is presented in the message. If done well, the whole worship experience is built around a theme and everything that is done connects to and reinforces that theme. This certainly includes the selection of music that relates to the message. It, of course, means the message is based on the Scripture selected and helps people take the principles presented in the Word and apply them to their daily lives. But it also includes creative ways of presenting the message so that we move beyond the standard lecture and reading methods. It includes interactive elements that encourage the participants to respond to what God is doing in their midst. It includes visual support (altar arrangements, banners, bulletins, etc.) that reinforces the message. It includes prayers and readings that tie into the message. It can even include the way in which participants greet each other.

For more information about the 4MAT process, go to www.aboutlearning.com. There are lots of great resources to help you get started.

> ### *Questions for Leaders and Coaches Related to Worship That Connects:*
>
> - Who is the target group for the worship experience? How does this form the way worship is designed?
> - In what ways is the preaching/teaching relevant to the everyday lives of people trying to honor God?
> - How are images and video included to support the message theme?
> - How is variety built into the weekly worship experiences to avoid a sense of routine?
> - How are people given an opportunity to respond to the message? Share some of your most exciting activities.
> - How much freedom does the pastor have (use) to move away from reading a prepared manuscript?
> - How are worship themes selected?
> - How is the proclamation of the Word supported by elements of worship beyond the preaching/teaching?
> - How is the theme of worship developed as the congregation

prepares for the worship experience or follows up on the worship experience?

- What opportunities exist in your worship for participants to take a next step in their discipleship journey?

WORSHIP DESIGN TEAMS

I remember the days clearly when I handed my secretary a form that indicated the hymns selected, Scripture reading, message title, and responsive readings so that she could put together the bulletin for Sunday morning. Thus concluded my "worship planning" for the week (except for writing the message of course)!

Worship design for me, and for pastors who are experiencing the amazing power of creative worship design, has come a long way. Most of that is due to the realization that we provide a much more creative, impactful, and engaging worship experience when a carefully selected team prepares it.

In my setting, the team included my assistant to the pastor (also a creative writing instructor and amazingly creative individual); my youth director (a great presenter in his own right and very creative thinker); a member of the praise team (especially aware of the resources in the music world); myself (a not-so-creative thinker but good organizer and worship leader/presenter). This core group was supplemented by: a technical support team, a visual design team (altar arrangements & banners), a drama team, and other music leaders, all of whom participated in worship planning based on availability and need. The full team also met once a month.

Drawing on the work of Len Wilson and Jason Moore in *Taking Flight with Creativity: Worship Design Teams That Work,* I would certainly include on this team a new believer if I were leading a team today. This would keep me from using language that is too churchy and concepts that are not understood by those beginning the faith journey.[8]

The creativity in the worship experience (both traditional and praise & worship) was a huge factor in the growth of that congregation over our years together. But it wasn't without effort and risk.

To be honest, we lost a few people when the church leadership decided to install the projection system in the sanctuary. A couple of people said they just couldn't worship where there was a screen (I referred them to a church where they would probably never install a screen). Being sensitive to the expectations of the more traditional worship services, we did not use the projection system or most of the creative elements used regularly in the praise services for nearly a year. Eventually, the participants in the traditional services asked for us to include these! The request came something like this: "How come you never do any of the cool stuff in our service that you do in the praise services?" At that point we knew the time was right.

Working with a worship team also takes more time and energy on the part of the pastor. But I promise you it is worth it and that you will see the results in the connections made in worship. I suggest planning message series several months in advance (titles, themes, Scriptures, and a brief paragraph indicating the direction the message is planned to take). This planning document is shared with the Creative Worship team, who begin to watch for illustrations, movie clips, stories, data, and resources around the themes. These are shared with the pastor in the weekly meetings.

A month out, the pastor provides the team with an outline of the message and proposed illustrations/other creative elements. The team begins to build the creative elements of the worship experience beyond the message.

Two weeks out, the team locks in the basic flow of the worship experience and has communicated special needs for video support (clips or creating a video), drama, visual arts, etc.

A week out, the pastor presents a draft of the message to the team for review. While this was initially a very intimidating experience, it was amazingly helpful. Often the team would suggest a better illustration or help change the language to something less churchy and easier to connect with.

A spreadsheet was prepared for each worship experience with every element identified and timed. The person responsible for leadership was identified and any special instructions for transitions described. During the service, the Assistant to the Pastor served as the Producer, making sure that everyone was ready for his or her role.

Every worship service included what I call the GPS focus:

- **G**od-centered: what God has done, who God is, what God is saying to us, what God is asking us to do or be, and where God is at work in our world.

- **P**articipatory: a focus on engaging people actively in the worship experience, giving them something to do, some way to respond to what God is doing in their midst.

- **S**ensory: finding ways to engage the senses, not just the brain. We tried to find ways to create visual connections, smells, tastes, touches that helped people engage the Word.

Questions for Leaders and Coaches Related to Worship Design Teams:

- How are the seasons of the church year and special events used to extend special invitations to the community?
- What options are you considering for worship as you look to future needs?
- What team(s) is/are in place to support the process of gathering for worship? How are they trained?
- What is the quality of printed materials distributed for worship? How are the materials designed to reflect an expectation that those unfamiliar with your worship experience might be present?
- How are worship themes selected?
- How does the design of the worship experience engage the next generation?
- Is the preaching/teaching relevant to the everyday lives of people trying to live as Jesus calls them?
- What role does a creative worship team play in the development of the message to be presented or in the focus on the Scriptures?
- How well does the service demonstrate a GPS focus: **God**-centered, **P**articipatory, and **S**ensory?

A word about corporate worship as training for worship as a lifestyle:

Think for a moment about all the things that are part of your regular worship experience. Name at least ten of them below:

You probably came up with some of the following, and probably some that are not identified here:

Prayer, Songs/Hymns, Offering, Message, Greeting, Scripture Reading, Response to the Word, Witness/Testimony, Benediction, Communion, Baptism, Responsive Readings, Altar Call/Time of Prayer, Announcements, Prayer Requests, Recognition of Visitors

These are all good things to do. They are also all ways that we can support worship participants in having a stronger worship lifestyle. For example:

- The Message: This is the easiest one. The message is a great opportunity to help people see the relevance of God's Word to their daily lives. We can give practical ways to live the way God intends for us.

- Prayer: For all of my years of ministry in the local church I offered an annual class on prayer. The problem was that only about 1% of the congregation participated and those were already our prayer warriors! Where does the rest of the congregation learn how to pray? With over 80% of regular worshipers wanting help in developing a personal relationship with Jesus, how do we help them if they don't come to a prayer class? I would suggest that the worship service gives us a great opportunity. What might be the result if we were to introduce a model of prayer (described in the bulletin, e.g. ACTS, ACTIP, the petitions of the Lord's Prayer) and then describe how that model would be used for the Pastoral Prayer? At the conclusion, the congregation would then be invited to try that prayer model for the next week.

- Scripture: Again, 80% of regular worshipers indicate through the research a need for learning how to study the Scriptures and apply them to daily life, but only a small percentage attend a Bible study. What if we were to introduce some easy Bible study tools as part of the Scripture presentation in worship: for example, a theological Bible study or reflective Bible study?

- Spiritual Disciplines: How might the congregation's connection to God be enhanced if we were to introduce them to things like praying the Scriptures or guided meditations or how to have a daily devotional time during the worship service?

- Offering: What if we, instead of just receiving the offering and providing an anthem, shared actual witnesses about the difference our sharing is making in the lives of those who give and/or those who receive? Sometimes we just need to help people connect the dots.

- Greeting: Even the greeting time can be a tool to help people see that hospitality is bigger than just saying "welcome to church." What if we were to encourage a real conversation and then ask them to continue that conversation following worship at the hospitality center?

The possibilities are endless. So is the difference it can make in the practice of a worship lifestyle.

Diagnosing the Level of Worship Engagement

Mystery Visitors: It is easy and inexpensive to have someone from outside the church visit the normal worship experience and then report on how they were welcomed and engaged by the event. Excellence in Ministry has a simple report form that is available at no cost (see www.emc3coaching.com).[9]

Real Discipleship Survey: This tool is designed for both individual use and as a congregational survey. It highlights the maturity level of individuals in several areas of the discipleship journey, including Worship. This tool is available from www.emc3coaching.com . For congregational use, the survey is taken by a representative group and then averaged in each of the dimensions of discipleship as an indicator of the level of maturity for the congregation as a whole.[10]

Congregational Survey: The measurement of worship practices as perceived by the congregation is part of a more comprehensive survey of congregational health. This is offered as both a pdf download and in a Survey Monkey format which gives an analysis (see www.emc3coaching.com).[11]

Discovering the Possibilities: This facilitated congregational workshop includes a variety of insights into the culture of worship extended by a congregation through congregational interview, discussion about missional vital signs, facility review, and the Real Discipleship Survey. Facilitator and Congregational Workshop materials are available through www.emc3coaching.com.[12]

Leadership Team Assessment: This document (available from www.emc3coaching.com) is a set of questions for local church leadership teams to consider. The practices of hospitality, worship, discipleship, service, and generosity are all included.[13]

Worship Survey: This document (a free resource available from www.emc3coaching.com) is a congregational survey providing insight into the experience of worshipers.[14]

Most of these and other tools are available in *Tips, Tools, and Activities for Coaching Church Leaders,* our companion resource for *Shift.* (See www.emc3coaching.com.)

Getting Started: Platform Stuff

In my work with congregations across the country, I have found several practices that are essential to the development of a culture of congregational worship. These do not represent the end-goal of worship; instead I have found that these are the foundations upon which a culture of passionate worship is built.

It Takes a Team

Congregations which consistently provide meaningful, creative, and relevant worship experiences have found that worship planning and execution is better accomplished by a team, often called the Creative Worship Team. This team can include staff members and must include the pastor but should also include members of the congregation (be sure to engage a new believer) who bring a level of creativity and perspective to the development process that is stronger than any one person alone.

The team ought to include representatives from those groups involved in executing worship (e.g. praise team, choir, etc.).

This process of designing worship does require some planning ahead as the pastor will need to have themes, Scriptures, and even thoughts about the direction of the message prepared well in advance.

Plan for GPS Worship

As you plan for worship, I encourage the use of a GPS model—God-centered, Participatory, and Sensory.

God-centered: The focus of worship is on what God has done, who God is, what God is saying to us, what God is asking us to do, and where God is at work in our world…or would like to be.

Participatory: Worship is not a spectator sport. People want to be included, involved in what is going on rather than just being passionate observers. How could your worship provide ways for people to participate?

Sensory: Much of worship tends to be from the eyebrows up, but we are more than just brains. We can touch and taste, see and smell, hear and feel emotions. What are some ways that your congregation has involved people's senses in worship?

Focus with a Single Unifying Theme

We believe the most powerful worship experiences are usually those that have a single, unifying theme. Life is complex—overwhelmingly so. People are bombarded with message after message all day long, all competing for their attention and none really getting it. The same thing can happen in worship. Consider all the competing messages people receive in any given worship service: several different announcements, songs that each have a message, prayers that communicate yet another message, special opportunities for service or giving, and then the Scripture and message, just to name a few.

Simple is in. Worship just works better when there is a unifying theme and everything done in worship helps build that theme. A good place to start is the worship service. Those who plan worship should be able to tell you the theme for every service, and everything in the service ought to serve that strategic focus.

Reinforce The Big Idea

Dave Ferguson, in a book entitled "The Big Idea" (a great read for worship teams) suggests that this idea of theming should go beyond even the worship event. If you really want people to get the big idea, reinforce it through a church-wide experience. He notes that the typical weekend worshiper is bombarded with nearly 20 different ideas during the worship experience.[15]

Some ways to accomplish this:

- Develop a study guide based on the theme of worship for use by Sunday school classes and small groups.
- Provide devotional thoughts for the week built around the worship theme.
- Give families the opportunity to share the theme together through family devotions.

- Give practical tips for living out the theme in real life (developing a worshipful lifestyle).

Present Important Truths in Unforgettable Ways

Studies show that people remember less than 10% of what they hear. That's why the unifying theme is so important—the message is presented in a variety of ways.

Use odd images, humor, video clips, witnesses, songs, skits, stories—use whatever you need to help people remember what you really want them to remember.

Make It Relevant

People are looking for practical ways to live out their faith. There is so much in Scripture that needs to be applied to people's everyday lives as they seek to live faithfully under the Lordship of Jesus Christ and to join him in service to others.

Too often in worship, there is discussion around word studies and historical facts that have absolutely nothing to do with where people live—no matter how interesting the preacher may find them. For people to sense God speaking to them in worship, they need to sense that what is being communicated has something to do with real life. If it doesn't, why use the gift of their time talking about it? Someone once told me, "Don't give them the recipe—serve the pie!"

Provide Practical Next Steps

People begin to build into their lives the behaviors that will form their attitudes and feelings as they are given solid next steps to take when leaving worship. It is important that worship leaders/preachers help people connect the dots—to see exactly what the message means in real, practical terms. In other words, how does one actually live into this?

What practical steps do people need to be challenged to take in the coming week to live into the theme of your worship?

Minimize Announcements

I know that this can be a touchy subject. But the truth is that announcements take over too many worship services. Here are two rules that can prevent this from happening:

- 3 in 3: This means that there are only three verbal announcements, and that they are made in just three minutes—either before or after the worship experience. Announcements should not be sprinkled throughout the worship service like advertisements in a TV show. You may get some flack about only having 3 announcements but most of the time they are already in the bulletin and people already know them. Put your announcements on PowerPoint slides as people are coming in to worship. Use creativity. But remember the rule: 3 in 3.

- 80% rule: If the announcement doesn't apply to 80% of the people in worship, don't waste everybody's time. Enough said.[16]

Pay Attention to Flow and Transitions

Flow and transitions are things that worship planners need to pay attention to if the worship service is going to feel right in today's world.

Flow has to do with how elements come together and lead one to the other. It has to do with things like not asking people to stand, then sit down, then stand back up right in a row. Bad flow. It also has to do with the emotional feeling of the different elements. You don't want people to feel like emotional yoyos.

Transition has to do with the logistics of moving from one element to another. When "Miss Emma" reads the Scripture and then sits down and then "Uncle John" stands up and walks slowly from the back of the church to make an announcement—that's a bad transition. When people speak, their microphone must be on. When there are video clips, they ought to work and start on cue.

The rule is that about 10 seconds of silence in a transition and you have lost the attention of the people. The more contemporary and/or creative worship services are, the more important it is for planners to give careful attention to flow and transitions.

Connect by Walking Around while Preaching

One of the most significant steps a pastor can take toward more fully engaging the congregation in worship is the movement away from notes and especially the reading of the message/sermon. Preaching while walking around produces a stronger connection with the congregation where there is a sense that you are talking from the heart and sharing directly with them.

I am not advocating a lack of preparation here. I suggest that the preacher still develop a full manuscript so that the message is well thought out. But the next step is to practice the delivery of the message so that you can do it without your notes.

Commit to Excellence

In today's world, especially for the younger generations, people have an expectation of excellence that is just part of the culture we live in. If what you do isn't done with excellence, then acting like it's just the church family can become a self-fulfilling act.

But think about it: is God glorified by mediocrity?

Suggested Resources for Coaches and Congregations Related to Worship:

- *The Big Idea: Aligning the Ministries of Your Church through Creative Collaboration,* Dave Ferguson, Zondervan, 2007

- *Taking Flight with Creativity: Worship Design Teams That Work,* Len Wilson & Jason Moore, Abingdon Press, 2009

- *Missional Worship: Increasing Attendance and Expanding the Boundaries of your Church,* Cathy Townley, Chalice Press, 2011

- *Toward Vitality Research Project,* Kim Shockley, General Board of Discipleship, 2012

- *Growing True Disciples: New Strategies for Producing Genuine Followers of Christ,* George Barna, WaterBrook Press, 2001

- *4MAT,* Dr. Bernice McCarthy, www.aboutlearning.com

shift 3:

From Membership to Discipleship

"I have been crucified with Christ and I no longer live,
but Christ lives in me."
The Apostle Paul, Galatians 2:20

"...so that we may no longer be children...
Rather, speaking the truth in love, we are to grow up
in every way into him who is the head, into Christ."
The Apostle Paul, Ephesians 4:14-15 (ESV)

"Come, follow me..."
Jesus, Matthew 4:19

"Therefore go and make disciples...teaching them to obey everything
I have commanded you."
Jesus, Matthew 28:19–20

Consider the following:

Jim and Sally were looking for a way to get connected in their new community. On Sunday morning they decided to start checking out the local churches. They visited "Grace Church" and really liked both the music and the pastor's message. At the end of the service an invitation was given. People could make a commitment to Jesus or renew their commitment to Jesus or, if they were ready, they could come forward and join the church.

Jim and Sally looked at each other and nodded. Then they walked up the aisle and became members of the congregation, giving their names to the pastor and saying yes to the stated vows.

In a church culture where the number of people on the rolls is the most important thing, this scenario might make sense. But it might explain why, in a large percentage of our congregations, only 25–40% of the membership actually attends worship in a given month or why so few people say that the church is actually relevant in their lives or why congregations become focused on taking care of "their own," rather than transforming their communities.

Of course most of our congregations don't just extend an open invitation like the one described above (although I have seen it done). We expect people to attend a "membership" class before they can join. Most commonly, this class runs between 2–4 hours and includes the following:

- an introduction to the pastor, staff, and key leaders
- an overview of the ministries of the church and explanation of how the church can serve those becoming members
- a brief history of the congregation/church
- an introduction to the history of the denomination with core beliefs, and of course...
- a pledge card for financial commitments

Again, in a church culture where it is all about getting people involved in the church and keeping people happy in the church, this all makes sense. This is a scenario being lived out in congregations all across the country. Our membership emphasis has become more about joining and feeling at home in our club, rather than expecting and helping members to grow as disciples of Jesus.

Observations about Discipleship

But the way I read our mission statement, none of this makes much sense. Consider the words of Jesus:

> "Therefore go and make disciples of all nations, baptizing them in the name of the Father and of the Son and of the Holy Spirit, and teaching them to obey everything I have commanded you" (Matthew 28:19–20).

Or the mission statement of the United Methodist Church:
To make disciples of Jesus Christ for the transformation of the world.[1]

Distinctions Between Membership and Discipleship

The church exists to "make disciples," not just "members." So what's the difference? Consider the following table and the distinctions made:

Members	Mature Disciples
Goal: Get people to join the congregation.	Goal: Create disciples who are increasing in their love of God and neighbor.
Church Role: Keep the members satisfied.	Church Role: Provide opportunities and relationships to foster spiritual growth.
Leadership Role: Encourage members to be involved in church activities.	Leadership Role: Encourage disciples to grow in obedience to God and service to others.
Responsibility for Growth: Church assumes primary responsibility for motivating people in their spiritual journey.	Responsibility for Growth: Disciples assume primary responsibility for spiritual growth as the church provides opportunities and encouragement.

One of the significant lessons I learned about halfway through my work as a "real pastor" (serving in a local congregation) was that to live out our mission (to make disciples) requires a shift in focus from membership to discipleship. Membership says, "It's about me." Discipleship says, "It's about God and others."

Membership Covenant

The starting point is providing clarity for those seeking to join the congregation about the role of the church and expectations of members. In my last appointment to a local congregation, our leadership team addressed this issue by the development of a *Membership Covenant*. It included the following commitments:

I will participate in weekly worship at least 3 weekends each month.

I will participate regularly in a small discipleship group or other accountable discipling relationship.

I will serve in some way in the local community (beyond the walls of the church) each month.

I will commit to proportional giving to the ministries of this congregation and to moving toward a tithe.

If I were helping develop this document today, I would include a commitment to bringing someone from outside the church to events (worship, small group, attractional ministries) three times a year and a commitment to build a relationship with at least three people outside of the church each year in order for them to experience the love of Christ in their lives.

As you have probably already noticed, these commitments are very consistent with the traditional membership vows:

Traditional Vows	Membership Covenant
Prayers	Participate regularly in a small discipleship group or other accountable discipling relationship.
Presence	Participate in weekly worship at least 3 weekends each month unless prevented by illness or travel.

Gifts	**Commit to proportional giving to the ministries of this congregation and to moving toward a tithe.**
Service	**Serve in some way in the local community (beyond the walls of the church) each month.**
Witness	**Invite someone to come with me to church/events at least three times per year and build at least three relationships outside the church to witness the love of Christ.**

The covenant agreement added some "meat to the bones," clarifying what our expectations were relative to the vows in that particular congregation.

You may be wondering if there was ever any push back about this clear set of commitments. The answer is yes.

I had a couple of times when, in a new member class as this was being presented, someone would say, "What if we're not ready for that level of commitment?"

My response went something like this: "That's OK. You've been attending here for 3 years now participating in worship. I visited you when you were in the hospital. I performed the baptism of your child. You join us regularly for fellowship dinners and special events. None of those things required you to be a member. In fact, I think you'll find no difference between the way you are loved and cared for and the way those who are members are loved and cared for..."

(You don't have to make the commitment, but if you do, this is what it means.)

Membership is not about how we will serve you. Membership is about a commitment to living as a disciple. The role of the church is to help you do that. It's about becoming part of a team (the body of Christ) that is seeking to make a difference in our world

It's all about making disciples. After all, that is why the church exists. It is our purpose.

However, while there is some specific discussion about building an intentional discipling process, the scope of what is presented points to the reality that everything we do as church needs to support the overarching purpose of making disciples.

Perspectives on Discipleship

Since our discussion is framed in this way, it is only fair to share some perspectives on what it means (from my point of view) to make mature disciples of Jesus Christ. The following are some of my thoughts.

Discipleship is about a lifestyle of worship. In a world where we are encouraged to meet our every need, desire, or hope—placing ourselves at the center of our world because "You're worth it," discipleship invites us to discover that true abundant life is the product of a life lived for God and others. Maturing disciples move away from "It's about me" and toward a lifestyle focused on God and others.

Discipleship is about relationships. Christianity is a relational faith. Our model is the Trinity—Father, Son, and Holy Spirit are One God, so intimately connected that they are each the full expression of the other. As Jesus put it in his prayer: "I pray....that all of them may be one, Father, just as you are in me and I am in you" (John 17:20–21) and "...When he, the Spirit of truth, comes...he will glorify me because it is from me that he will receive what he will make known to you. All that belongs to the Father is mine. That is why I said the Spirit will receive from me what he will make known to you" (John 16:13–15).

Like the fullness of the relationship modeled in the Trinity, disciples are called to be in relationship with God (Father, Son, and Holy Spirit), with each other, and with the world that God loves. It is this calling that is expressed so clearly in the traditional communion liturgy prayer: "*Make us one with Christ, one with each other, and one in our ministry to all the world.*"[2]

Not only is discipleship about relationships, it is formed in relationships. The Scriptures are replete with examples of this understanding about making disciples: Jesus and the disciples, Barnabas and Paul, Paul and Timothy, Elijah and Elisha, Moses and Joshua, and the list goes on.

These relationships are characterized by commitment to one another, transparency, discovery, encouragement, challenge, accountability, and love. They are a model worthy of our focus and attention today as well.

Discipleship is about a process, not a program. John Wesley, founder of the Methodist movement, asked the question that continues to be asked of every candidate for ordination in the United Methodist Church: "Are you going on to perfection?" By perfection, he does not mean absolute perfection (that only works for Jesus) but a perfect love for God and others. I'm not sure why this question is asked only to those seeking ordination, since we are all ordained by our baptism and we are all called to move toward maturity as disciples. This idea of "movement" is critical to the process of discipleship. Discipleship is not a state of being. It is a process of becoming.

For the past few decades the model used for making disciples has been predominantly programmatic. Drawing on the work of Greg Ogden in *Transforming Discipleship,* consider the following set of distinctions:

- As a process supported by relationships, discipleship is about investing in people so that the life of Jesus is integrated into their being. As a program, discipleship is safe, controllable, and less intrusive. It largely substitutes information for investing in people.

- As a process, discipling relationships have a full, mutual responsibility. As a program, one or a few do on behalf of the many.

- As a process, discipling relationships are customized to the unique growth of the individual. As a program, discipleship emphasizes synchronization and regimentation.

- As a process, discipling relationships focus accountability on life change. As a program, accountability focuses on understanding or retention of content.[3]

Discipleship is about engaging our world. Rick Rusaw and Eric Swanson made the questions, "If your church vanished, would your community weep? Would anyone notice? Would anyone care?" a catchphrase for congregations all across the country. The message is clear: the church doesn't exist to serve us; it exists to serve the world—to transform the world.[4]

To be a disciple and to equip people to be growing in maturity as disciples includes developing a heart, a passion, for serving others. This may take a variety of forms. It may be a personal ministry to a neighbor or friend or co-worker. It may be through participation in teams providing community service. It may be accomplished through leadership in community organizations or support of recreational activities for children and youth in the community. It may be through regular participation in short-term mission experiences for disaster relief or the development of physical support to third-world nations. It may be through providing financial resources to meet the needs of those less fortunate or for those serving others.

The effective, vital congregation helps disciples discern their gifting, passions, and calling for making a difference.

Discipleship is about becoming like Jesus. This is different from learning about Jesus. It is about transformation, not education. Real discipleship is about behaviors. Let's consider some observations about discipleship based on current research and experience working with congregations in transformation:

- Recent research indicates that there is little to no difference in the behaviors of those who call themselves "born again" Christians and those who are non-believers.

- Young adults, in particular, have a very negative perspective on the faithfulness of Christians in reflecting the life and worldview of Jesus.

- The driving factors in maturing discipleship are personal relationships and accountable discipleship.

- The longing for a strong spiritual connection is significant in the culture as a whole. This does not get translated into participation in a traditional community of faith.

- The educational model coming out of the modern era has proved ineffective in creating real disciples.

- There is no "one size fits all" approach to discipleship. People have differing needs for relationships and accountability at different points along the journey.

- Discipleship is a lifelong journey. No one retires from becoming a disciple.

When coaching the congregation in the area of discipleship all of these observations come into play. The goal is to help the congregation consider how it might support the development of mature disciples who reflect the behaviors and worldview of Jesus.

Over the years, particularly coming out of the modern scientific era, discipleship ministries have been based on the core definition of a disciple as a "learner." This was easy and convenient. We could "teach" about what it means to be a disciple. So the Church developed a very academic approach to equipping disciples. Yearlong treks through the Bible became the norm. For those who wanted to dig deeper, there were verse-by-verse studies of particular books. Then we added themed studies around topics that could help people understand how to live as better disciples.

So, here we are in the post-modern era and a number of studies have been done to see how all this focus on learning and teaching has worked (e.g. George Barna or The Fermi Project).

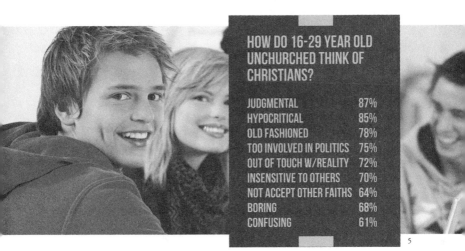

HOW DO 16-29 YEAR OLD UNCHURCHED THINK OF CHRISTIANS?

JUDGMENTAL	87%
HYPOCRITICAL	85%
OLD FASHIONED	78%
TOO INVOLVED IN POLITICS	75%
OUT OF TOUCH W/REALITY	72%
INSENSITIVE TO OTHERS	70%
NOT ACCEPT OTHER FAITHS	64%
BORING	68%
CONFUSING	61%

5

The answer: It didn't!

We missed the part of the definition of disciple as learner that focused on actually becoming like Jesus, not just learning about Jesus.

So, let's be clear…

- Discipleship is not just about learning about Jesus. It is about *becoming like* Jesus.
- Discipleship is not just about education. It is about *transformation*.
- Discipleship is not just about knowledge. It is about *behaviors*.

A Theology of Discipleship

Our mission is to make disciples of Jesus Christ for the transformation of the world. This clearly points us in a direction away from ourselves. That is very different from the idea of making members, where the focus is on what we get out of the deal: "What's in it for us?" and, "How will you meet my needs?" The Shift from Membership to Discipleship invites congregations to refocus their energies on the mission. The goal is the development of maturing disciples who are increasing in love of God and neighbor—growing in obedience to God and in service to others.

A Definition of Discipleship

We suggest that discipleship be described as:

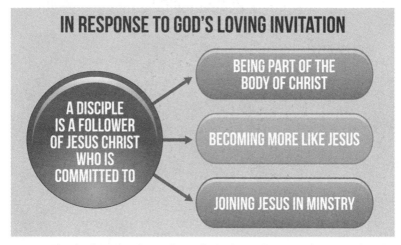

One way to look at this focus through the lens of Scripture is found in the familiar words of Jesus:

> *Follow me (being part of the body of Christ)*
> *I will make you (becoming more like Jesus)*
> *Fishers of men (joining Jesus in ministry)* (Matthew 4:19 RSV)

It is important to note that for each of these three areas presented it is not identified how the person will live that out. Discipleship is a very personal journey and what works for one person will not necessarily work for another.

There is no "disciple-in-a-box"!

However, there are several dimensions of discipleship that relate to these three broad strokes identified in the definition.

Consider the following depiction. This indicates dimensions of the discipleship journey that relate to that particular area.

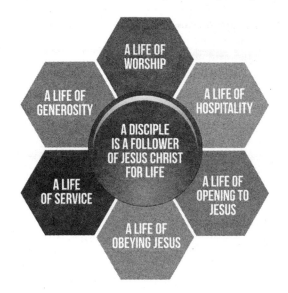

In **being part of the Body of Christ** locally, we live a life of worship and a life of hospitality.

> A life of **worship** includes participation in corporate worship, as well as personal worship (e.g. devotional time) and even a life-style of worship where every action and circumstance becomes an opportunity to give glory to God.

> A life of **hospitality** includes being part of the church community and welcoming new people to worship. It also includes our interpersonal relationships with and our acceptance of people who are outside the church and quite unlike us—even to the point of intentionally building relationships with persons beyond the church in order to embody Christ's love.

In **becoming more like Jesus,** we live a life opening to Jesus and increasingly obeying what Jesus has taught us. Together these reflect Intentional Discipling.

> A life of **Opening to Jesus** includes not only hearing sermons that teach the Scriptures, studying Scripture, and reading Scripture devotionally, but also engaging in those spiritual practices that develop our awareness of the presence of God. As followers mature

in this dimension, they take more and more responsibility for their own spiritual development and become less dependent upon the institution for their growth.

A life of **Obeying Jesus** involves becoming more like Jesus in our actions, attitudes and responses to others. It begins with the acceptance of a relationship with Jesus and a commitment to growth as a disciple. We not only develop a Christian worldview in our daily living, but we also increasingly come to embody the example and teachings of Jesus. Jesus is Lord over all aspects of our life. Maturity in this dimension involves partnering with someone beginning the journey and helping them develop as a disciple of Jesus.

In **joining Jesus in ministry,** we live a life of service and a life of generosity.

A life of **service** includes supporting the ministry of the local church with our time and energy and participating in service projects sponsored by the church, but it also includes a lifestyle investing the best of who we are in service to others.

A life of **generosity** certainly includes presenting our tithes and offerings as an act of worship, but it also includes creating a lifestyle with margins that allow us to respond to the needs of others God puts in our path on a daily basis.

As you probably recognize, these dimensions of discipleship are directly related to the membership covenant discussed previously:

Traditional Vows	Dimensions of Discipleship	Membership Covenant
Prayers	Opening to Jesus/ Obeying Jesus	Participate regularly in a small discipleship group or other accountable discipling relationship.
Presence	A Life of Worship	Participate in weekly worship at least 3 weekends each month unless prevented by illness or travel.

Gifts	A Life of Generosity	Commit to proportional giving to the ministries of this congregation and to moving toward a tithe.
Service	A Life of Service	Serve in some way in the local community (beyond the walls of the church) each month.
Witness	A Life of Hospitality	Invite someone to come with me to church/events at least three times per year and build at least three relationships outside the church to witness the love of Christ.

Discipleship as a Journey

The Apostle Paul urges us to grow into maturity or completeness. John Wesley uses the language of "Christian Perfection."

Whichever way we look at it, from the very beginning discipleship has been a journey toward the fullness of life that is offered to us in Jesus Christ. This journey happens in stages of development very similar to our life stages. In fact, this is the very language that Jim Putman uses in *Real Life Discipleship*:

- Pre-stage (not yet "born again")
- Infancy
- Childhood
- Adolescent/Young Adult
- Parenthood/Adult[6]

It doesn't take a lot of imagination to see the connections to the journey in faith. In infancy, we are exploring everything. The whole world is new and we're amazed by what we're experiencing. But we're not really engaged except to be cute and cuddly.

In the childhood phase we are all about learning about our world. We don't know much, if anything, and someone has to guide us along—teach us the language, keep us from doing things that will hurt us, and help us to develop in ways that will be the foundations for the rest of life.

The adolescent phase moves us into taking responsibility for our lives. We begin to establish some independence. We discover what works well for us. We make some of our own decisions about how to do life.

The parenthood/adult phase moves us squarely into the realm of focusing beyond ourselves. We realize that life done well is done so by helping others do life well. We continue to grow personally, but the focus becomes other-centered.

We use the language of Searching, Exploring, Beginning, Growing, and Maturing to describe these phases of development as a disciple:

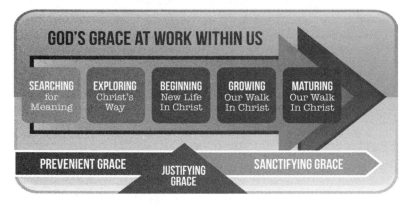

The phases might be described as:

Searching (pre-life in Christ): All persons seek to make sense of their life asking questions like "What gives my life purpose, joy, and fulfillment?" They may seek to fill this fundamental need many different ways. (See Acts 17:22f)

Exploring (infancy): May attend church and want to belong, but they have not yet committed to following Jesus. They may wrestle intellectually with God's presence in their life, often with more caution than curiosity. The longer they attend, however, the less likely they are to commit. (See John 1:45f)

Beginning (childhood): Growing to understand and put their newfound faith into practice. Growth can be awkward. They are often vulnerable to insecurity and doubt. They are also the most excited about their faith. This is the largest and most active segment in church activities. (See Matthew 7:24f)

Growing (adolescent): Eager to be identified as Christians and are going public with their faith. They are increasingly willing to take responsibility for their growing relationship with Jesus. They seek to integrate their faith into life in a holistic way and look to Jesus to help them live their life. (See Ephesians 4:14f)

Maturing (parents): This group is moving toward complete surrender of their lives to Jesus. They exist to know, love, obey, serve, and be with Jesus. They also realize that the role of a disciple is to help make other disciples and live life with that focus. (See Galatians 2:20f)

It is important to note here that not only are there phases of development and that people in the congregation will find themselves in different phases, but also that the various dimensions of the life of a disciple will often reflect differing levels of maturity. For example, a person may have a great passion for serving others and a well-developed sense of calling (maturing phase for service) but may be in the beginning phase for opening to Jesus. They have made a commitment to be a disciple but have not moved into a growing relationship. Often the service dimension can serve as a catalyst for growth in other areas.

A friend of mine (we'll call him Jack) is an American contractor who lives out of country where he runs a construction business. Jack and I got connected through a seemingly obscure relational connection through a mission organization (ReGenesis Ministries) for which I provide leadership. Jack is what one might describe as "a little rough around the edges" (maybe a lot!). He is a lapsed Catholic and former drug addict. Yet, every time I take a mission team to that area, Jack takes the week off from his business and arranges supplies for the project, provides equipment for the team, and even trains the team for the needs of the project.

During those team experiences, Jack also goes to church, attends daily devotional times, makes sure that we pray for every meal, and announces to everybody we meet that "This is my preacher friend from the States."

Jack is a perfect example of one who is more developed in one area than in another. We suggest that you build on the strengths. With Jack it took several trips before he began to respond to anything "spiritual" or "religious." Over the years he has come a long way. Now he even invites his friends to go to church with us!

Relational Support for the Discipleship Process

Discipleship happens in relationships! I'm not sure why, but we seem to have moved away from this understanding and substituted for it an educational model rather than supplementing discipleship with Christian Education.

Jesus didn't say, "Take a class." He said, "Come, follow me." Discipleship is personal and relational.

The genius of John Wesley, founder of the Methodist movement, was that of building a process for discipleship based on different levels of relationship. The following diagram depicts that process:

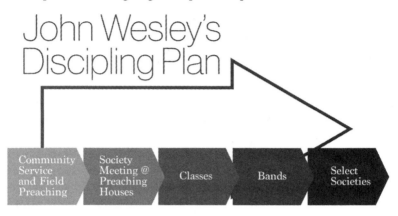

When people were exploring the faith, they were invited to a society meeting (basically a worship service) where they could come to an understanding of why it was important to be a disciple of Jesus.

As persons began their commitment as a disciple of Jesus, they were required to participate (if they wanted to be Methodists) in a "Class Meeting." This was a larger group format led by a spiritual leader with weekly meetings designed to teach the basics of the faith and hold people accountable for their progress in living as disciples.

The most mature of the "Class Meeting" group were invited to participate in "bands." These were much smaller groups (4–5) of the same gender who engaged, under the leadership of a spiritual coach, in a much more intense focus on faith training and accountability.

The best of the "bands" were selected for one-on-one training in faith development and leadership and were prepared to become leaders of societies, classes, and bands.

The following paradigm provides a model for building the same kind of focus on relationships and accountability into our more contemporary setting:

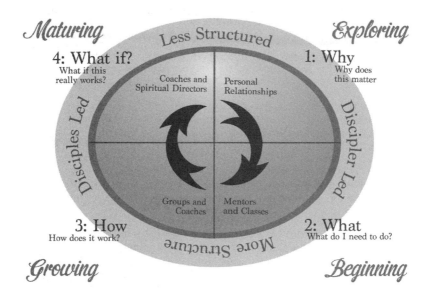

Let's take this diagram section by section:

Note the two major axes. The vertical axis divides the image into right and left halves. On the right are found the two phases of development during which more support is needed. We call these "discipler led." This means, of course, that since people in these phases of development have not yet built a foundation, they will need someone to lead them—either through personal conversation or through a class.

On the left side of the image are the two phases of development that represent people who have built the foundations and are moving into an ever-maturing relationship with Jesus. We call this half "disciple led" because the support needed is determined by the disciple.

The horizontal axis divides the image into top and bottom halves. The upper portion is "less structured," which means it is not based on formal classes or groups. The bottom half is "more structured," which means that the disciples in this part of the journey are best served by a more structured environment such as classes and small groups or a formal mentoring or coaching relationship.

The image is divided into four quadrants, each representing a phase of development. Let's look at each quadrant individually.

The exploring quadrant represents people who are checking out a faith relationship with Jesus (see discipleship matrix). They are usually asking some form of the question "Why?" or "Why does this matter?" They do not have a commitment level for participation in a small group and may not find the answers they are looking for in that environment anyway. They are best served in one-on-one relationships where someone from the church (sponsor, coach, etc.) partners with them to help explore what a discipling relationship looks like and whether it is right for them.

Since those who are exploring the Christian life usually come to that point through relationships with those who are already believers (e.g. the story of Nathanael and Philip from John's Gospel), they need to be received well. If they show up at a worship service to check things out, being received well includes the excellence with which the service is conducted, the relevance of the message to their daily lives, and the witness to a commitment by this congregation to engage the community and make a difference.

In helping people move toward a life committed to being a disciple of Jesus Christ, research has shown that there are several catalysts that are most influential:

Top 5 Things Those Exploring Want from the Church as Identified by Willow Creek:

- Help developing a personal relationship with Christ (68%)
- Compelling worship services (68%)
- A feeling of belonging (68%)
- Help understanding the Bible (67%)
- Church leaders who model spiritual growth (66%)[7]

Questions for Leaders and Coaches Related to Exploring Christ's Way:

- How are newcomers engaged by someone from the congregation?
- How are spiritual conversations encouraged for the development of understanding key Christian beliefs?
- What system is in place to help newcomers find a way to serve in a ministry?
- How are new believers introduced to the practice of reflecting on Scripture?
- What kinds of opportunities are provided for the building of relationships?
- On a scale of 1–10, how applicable is the worship message to daily life?
- How does this congregation witness to its engagement of the surrounding community?
- How are members of the congregation encouraged to be engaged with those beyond the walls of the church?
- What support is offered by the church for inviting peers, friends, family, and neighbors to worship?
- How is the worship experience designed to invite people to take a next step in their faith journey?
- What is the practice of this congregation in following up with newcomers?
- What is the trend in "professions of faith" for this congregation?

BEGINNING PHASE

The beginning quadrant represents people who have made a commitment to be a disciple of Jesus. The question they are asking is "What?" or "What's it all about?" They are usually seeking help building the foundations of that relationship. This group is best served by providing introductory classes in the faith (e.g. *Alpha*) and foundational classes in discipleship practices (e.g. *Following Jesus, Foundations, A Disciple's Path*). Larger groups work well since this is primarily educational in focus. For smaller churches, having mentors from the congregation willing to work one-on-one with beginners in the journey seems to work well.

The beginning phase of discipleship is often accompanied by a sense of excitement as believers begin a new journey in life. It is also a time when there is a great deal of uncertainty about how to live into this new calling. The church has an amazing opportunity to help provide a foundation for this new life in Christ.

To help disciples who have begun life as a disciple move toward a deeper relationship with Jesus and a greater sense of God's presence in daily life, research has shown the following catalysts to be most influential:

Top 5 Things Those Beginning Want from the Church as Identified by Willow Creek:

- Help developing a personal relationship with Christ (83%)
- Help in understanding the Bible in greater depth (82%)
- Church leaders who model spiritual growth (78%)
- Compelling worship experiences (75%)
- Challenge to grow and take next steps (74%)[8]

Questions for Leaders and Coaches Related to Beginning a New Life in Christ:

- How does this congregation celebrate with people who have made a decision to follow Jesus?
- What kinds of connections are provided to help people discover what this new life will look like for them?
- How does the worship service equip people with tools for strengthening personal worship?
- What kind of training is provided for building the foundations of spiritual practices?
- How are people invited to be in some form of discipling relationship beyond the worship experience?
- What types of "on-ramp" service/mission experiences are available to help people discover the joy of service?
- How does this congregation help people discover their gifts and passions for ministry?

GROWING PHASE

The growing phase represents people who are moving into a more committed relationship with Jesus. They are asking the question "How?" or "How does it work?" We have moved into the "disciple led" portion of the journey where the equipping of disciples becomes much more personal and individualized. Not everybody has the same needs. Some will want to explore more advanced spiritual practices and others will long for a deeper understanding of how God is calling them to be in service to the community. In this quadrant we move from a one-size-fits-all to a more coach-like approach. Small groups tend to be the cornerstone of this phase of development, giving the opportunity for deeper exploration. We have also found that discipleship coaching is a powerful tool in working with this group.

Those in the growing phase of discipleship have begun to realize that there is more to the journey than just showing up for worship and having a daily devotional time. There is a longing for a deeper relationship with Jesus, a stronger sense of the presence of God in daily life, and a growing commitment to make a difference in the world.

Top 5 Things Those Growing Want from the Church as Identified by Willow Creek:

- Help in understanding the Bible in greater depth (90%)
- Help in developing a personal relationship with Christ (89%)
- Church leaders who model spiritual growth (87%)
- Challenge to grow and take next steps (84%)
- Encouragement to take personal responsibility for
- spiritual growth (84%)[9]

Questions for Leaders and Coaches Related to Growing Our Walk in Christ:

- How is the congregation introduced to spiritual practices through the worship experiences?

- What types of relationships are available to support people in their growth toward maturity?

- What classes are offered that invite participants to explore the spiritual disciplines?

- How does this congregation connect people with a variety of service/mission opportunities?

- How are people equipped to use their financial resources in ways that honor God?

- In what ways does the congregation encourage cross-cultural and cross-ethnic understanding and relationships?

- What opportunities are offered to the congregation to develop missional connections within other cultures?

- Is there a clear picture of what maturity as a disciple looks like for this congregation?

As you may have noted, in all of the "top five" factors identified by Willow Creek, the focus on Scripture reflection was a significant component.

Get People in the Word

Regular biblical reflection is the "vanilla ice cream" of spiritual growth. You can put all kinds of things on top of the vanilla ice cream, but the ice cream is what builds the foundation. Notice that this is biblical reflection, not just reading the Scriptures.

There are lots of ways to encourage the reading of Scripture. Provide a daily reading plan (perhaps related to sermon/message topics) for your congregation. Direct people to a reading plan through a link on your website. Provide copies of the *Upper Room* for your congregation.[10]

Teach people how to have a daily devotional time that includes the reading of and reflection on Scriptures. Basic tools like the Reflective Bible Study or Theological Bible Study methods are very helpful.

Start every meeting, group session, dinner, worship experience, or service experience with a devotional based on Scripture. Invite people to reflect on what God is saying through the Word about their lives, the life of the congregation, and their call to be the Church for the world.

Encourage people to bring their Bibles to church and to highlight, underline, circle, or make notes as God brings life to the printed Word.

MATURING PHASE

The maturing phase represents people who are moving toward being "sold out" to Jesus. They are longing to continue their growth, but also have a commitment to help others discover the blessings they are experiencing. They are asking the question "What If?" or "What if I became a fully devoted disciple?" seeking to go wherever God leads them. The strongest relational support for this group is the discipleship coach or a spiritual director as needed. This phase of growth requires much less relational structure.

In the maturing phase of development as a disciple, the focus turns toward equipping people to be disciplers of others. It is a movement toward understanding that it is not about "me" or "my development" but how God can use the maturity in our faith journey to encourage and support others as they grow toward maturity.

Questions for Leaders and Coaches Related to Moving Toward Maturity:

- What kinds of training are available to support mature disciples in mentoring, sponsoring, and/or coaching beginners in the discipleship journey?
- Who is available to support the continuing development of maturing disciples (e.g. discipleship coaches, spiritual directors)?
- What activities are supported by the congregation to encourage the development of maturing disciples?
- How are mature disciples identified and invited to serve in leadership roles within the congregation?

Diagnosing the Level of Discipleship

In addition to the coaching questions described, there are a variety of tools available to assist the coach in determining the level of discipleship offered within a congregation. For example:

- *Discipleship Groups/Accountable Discipling Relationships Data:* The percentage of the congregation involved in discipleship groups is reported by congregations in terms of the numbers of people actively engaged in small groups. This data is readily available, but a more accurate picture would also include those in accountable discipling relationships (mentoring, coaching, spiritual direction). While this is certainly not the only indicator of discipleship, this data does point the coach toward the health expressed in the most common form of discipleship.

- *Real Discipleship Survey:* This survey instrument (available from www.emc3coaching.com) is used as both a personal growth instrument and as a tool to survey the maturity levels of the congregation in six dimensions of the discipleship journey. The latter is helpful in assisting congregations to see areas of need that might be supported by the congregation.[11]

- *Congregational Survey:* The measurement of discipleship practices as perceived by the congregation is part of a more comprehensive survey of congregational health. This is offered as both a pdf download and in a Survey Monkey format which gives an analysis (www.emc3coaching.com)[12]

- *Leadership Team Assessment:* This document (available from www.emc3coaching.com) is a set of questions for local church leadership teams to consider. The practices of hospitality, worship, discipleship, service, and generosity are all included.[13]

Most of these and other tools are available in *Tips, Tools, and Activities for Coaching Church Leaders,* our companion resource for *Shift.* (See www.emc3coaching.com.)

Getting Started: Platform Stuff

In my work with congregations across the country, I have found several practices that are essential to the development of a culture of congregational discipleship. These do not represent the end-goal of discipleship. Instead, I have found that these are the foundations upon which a culture of discipleship is built.

Clarify Your Discipling Process

This requires being clear about what a disciple is and does—and then designing environments in which people, with the help of the Holy Spirit, are most likely to move in that direction. Unless your church leaders know the goal and the route your congregation is taking to get there, the likelihood of people becoming mature apprentices of Jesus is slim.

To fulfill the mission of Christ, it is critical for congregational leaders to clearly and regularly communicate what they hope for each person spiritually.

A pathway outlining how the congregation is prepared to support people in their spiritual journey is also important.

Suppose someone visiting your congregation asks you, "So what does it mean to be a disciple of Jesus Christ and how will this congregation help me do that?" What will you say?

Host a Congregational Information Meeting

It used to be that every church, especially in the same denominational brand, was about the same. Not so today—and that's good, because communities are very different. Many people have no idea what it means to be a Christian, much less a Wesleyan Christian. Many people have no more idea what happens in a church than most of us raised in the Christian church know what happens in a Buddhist Temple. Visitors need to get a sense of what your congregation stands for, where it is headed, and whether they personally will be welcomed. What does your congregation hope for them spiritually and how are you going to assist them to realize these hopes?

How do your leaders communicate the answers to these questions to persons who are considering being part of your congregation?

Offer Foundations/Membership Classes

It used to be that you could assume most people understood the basics of the Christian faith. Maybe this was always an inaccurate assumption to make, but these days it is a documented reality. For example, the reason that many people don't join in the Lord's Prayer during weddings is…they don't know it! It is recommended that the Foundations Class be done in place of the traditional membership class. It is a starting point for those beginning the discipleship journey and much more relevant than the typical "get to know the church and denomination" class!

People don't need to be seminary-trained to be disciples, but there are some basic things they need to know and understand:

- What do Christians believe?
- How do I read Scripture?
- How do I pray?
- How do I cultivate a life of devotion?
- How do I relate to others in Christ?
- How do I manage my finances biblically?

- How has God wired me up to serve?
- What opportunities are there for me to serve others using my gifts?

What does your congregation do to help new members learn these basics?

Everyone in a Discipling Relationship

While Jesus preached and taught and healed among the masses, he poured most of his time into a small group of followers. The truth is that a small group of less than a dozen people who together are seeking to be Jesus' apprentices is the foundational relationship for nurturing spiritual growth in most churches.

Each group needs to be balanced around 1) developing caring relationships, 2) developing a closer walk with Christ through study, prayer, and teaching, and 3) being involved as a group serving beyond themselves on a regular basis.

Each small discipling group needs to have a spiritually mature and trained leader and to be using curriculum selected to advance persons in their spiritual journey. To support this process if there are not sufficient mature and trained leaders, it is essential that leaders be in a relationship for development and training. This may be done by the pastor or by a couple of mature disciples.

Of course, small groups are not the only alternative for providing discipling relationships. Your congregation might consider one-on-one or triad discipling relationships, mentoring relationships, discipleship coaching relationships, or spiritual direction relationships, or some combination of the above.

What percentage of your average worshipers is involved in discipling relationships? How do you go about selecting and training leaders? Would people say that being part a discipling relationship is a basic expectation for all members?

Every Six Months, Help Disciples Review Their Spiritual Growth and Plan Next Steps

This may come as a surprise to many people, especially if you grew up in a church where attending several times a month, making a financial pledge, and being a decent person were about all that was expected (or hoped for, either). Our recommendation is that congregations organize so that every disciple who wishes has the opportunity to sit down with a more mature disciple twice a year for a conversation focused on their spiritual journey.

How is it going with you spiritually? How can we better support you as you grow to become a fully devoted follower of Jesus Christ? What are your next steps at this point in your journey?

What do you think the effect of doing this for people in your congregation would be?

Close the Back Door

Some congregations are great at welcoming people initially, but very soon it seems these same persons attend less and less, and then only at Christmas Eve and Easter. They have slipped out the back door—often because they didn't feel connected or engaged in the congregation.

Closing the back door may involve different things in different congregations. At the very least, it involves caring enough about people that you track their attendance and participation. If someone begins to miss worship, you can then contact him or her, let them know you have missed them, and ask if everything is all right.

As you connect with people, listen for patterns that may suggest a problem in your discipling process. For example, one congregation began to recognize that new people weren't getting involved in small discipling groups where they could make new friends. Consequently these persons felt like they never belonged. The congregation implemented several strategies for helping persons make the transition from worship to small groups. Another congregation discovered that newcomers liked the pastor but found that longtime members, although nice enough, didn't really make people feel welcomed.

Are your leaders tracking people's participation so that you can recognize if and when they are slipping out the back door? If you were to talk with those slipping out the back door, what might you discover is the reason for their disappointment and/or sense of disengagement?

Suggested Resources for Coaches and Congregations Related to Discipleship:

- *Simple Church: Returning to God's Process for Making Disciples,* Thom S. Rainer and Eric Geiger, B&H Books, 2011
- *Foundations,* Phil Maynard
- *Deepening Your Effectiveness: Restructuring the Local Church for Life Transformation,* Dan Glover and Claudia Lavy, Discipleship Resources, 2006

- *A Disciple's Path: Deepening Your Relationship with Christ and the Church,* James A. Harnish, Abingdon Press, 2012
- *Disciple: Getting Your Identity from Jesus,* Bill Clem, Crossway, 2011
- *The Disciple Making Church: From Dry Bones to Spiritual Vitality,* Gordon McDonald, FaithWalk Publishing, 2004
- *Growing True Disciples: New Strategies for Producing Genuine Followers of Christ,* George Barna, WaterBrook Press, 2001
- *Transforming Discipleship: Making Disciples a Few at a Time,* Greg Ogden, IVP Books, 2003
- *Following Jesus: Steps to a Passionate Faith*, Carolyn Slaughter, Abingdon Press, 2008

shift 4:

From "Serve Us" to Service
(Internal Focus to External Focus)

"Lord, when did we see you hungry or thirsty or a stranger or needing clothes or sick or in prison, and did not help you?" He will reply, " Truly I tell you, whatever you did not do for one of the least of these, you did not do for me."
Jesus, Matthew 25:44–45

"The world hears the Gospel when it sees it, when its witnesses are clearly committed to a more fully human future, in this world and the next." [1]
Albert Outler, Methodist Theologian

"If your congregation suddenly disappeared, would the community mourn losing the blessings they provide?"
Erick Swanson, *The Externally Focused Church* [2]

In 2004 I was living and serving a local church in the South Orlando area in Florida (near Disney World). After several years of little impact from hurricanes, it seemed our time was due. In the span of just a few weeks, Central Florida was hit with three major storms back-to-back (Charley, Frances, and Jeanne), all of them crossing right through our community.

Everywhere you looked following each storm trees were down, blocking roads and driveways; roofs had large sections of shingles blown off. creating major leaks inside many homes; and to top it off, thousands were without power.

In this relatively upscale community, people definitely came to church with the questions, "What do you have for me? For my children? For my youth?" Much emphasis had been placed on excellence in everything that was done. After all, they deserved nothing but the best. (This was the Disney World area after all!)

The most amazing thing happened following the storms. With the power out in homes all around the community, a group from the church got together and fixed coffee and sandwiches to take around the neighborhoods. Teams got together and went from home to home to put blue tarps over the damaged roofs. Other teams got together and took their chainsaws and cut up the trees blocking roads and driveways.

It was a pivotal moment in the life of this congregation. It went from a perspective of "serve us" to "service." That event began a focus on ministry in the community serving those less fortunate and acted as a catalyst for the beginning of mission team support to other regions of the country, and even to Honduras and Jamaica.

Observations about Service

Service is about joining Jesus in ministry to the world, using our gifts and graces to engage others in ways that bring hope, healing, and wholeness to life. Let's consider some observations about service in local congregations based on current research and my work with congregations in transformation:

- We live in a culture where, as Albert Outler puts it, "The world hears the Gospel when it sees it, when its witnesses are clearly committed to a more fully human future, in this world and the next" (as quoted by Lovett Weems).[3]

- Our mission is to make disciples of Jesus Christ for the transformation of the world.

- Engagement in the ministries of serving others is often the entry point for people (especially our young adults) into the life of a congregation.

- Many congregations (in our experience, a strong majority), engage in acts of generosity by providing resources to organizations while calling them "service."

- Service is an integral part of our growth as disciples of Jesus Christ.

One of the realities of the *Toward Vitality* research done by several of the Methodist General Agencies is that most of the 158 congregations that were interviewed experienced significant positive change by shifting their focus from inward to outward. This changed the way the congregants related to their pastor (and staff), as they learned that the pastor is not there to serve them, but to equip them to be in mission and ministry. This shift in thinking also caused congregants to look at their community with a sense of God's purposes, as opportunities rather than difficulties.[4]

A Theology of Service

Rick Rusaw and Eric Swanson made the questions, "If your church vanished, would your community weep? Would anyone notice? Would anyone care?"—a catchphrase for congregations all across the country.[5] The message is clear: the church doesn't exist to serve us, it exists to serve the world—to transform the world. This shift from "serve us" to service invites the church to consider how this dimension of discipleship is supported by the congregation—from helping disciples explore giftedness and passions to providing opportunities for engaging in various levels of service.

From the call of Abram to be a blessing to all peoples (Genesis 12) to the admonition of Jesus that when we clothe the naked, feed the hungry, and give drink to the thirsty we serve him (Matthew 25), the people of God have been charged with serving those in need.

To be a disciple is to be a servant. To be a church is to serve. The church cannot be the church without being missional in nature.

But this service to the last and the least among us is greater than giving a handout. It is common to find congregations that provide resources to other organizations who serve those in need. We provide backpacks for children going to school, food for community food pantries, peanut butter sandwiches for children needing nourishment over the weekend between school days, clean socks for the shelter serving the homeless, Angel tree gifts for children at Christmas, and turkey dinners for those in need on Thanksgiving.

These are all great things and we should support those serving the ones in need. But they are what I call missional gestures. They provide resources that are needed, but without our involvement in the lives of those in need—without "getting our hands dirty." I believe that every congregation should have a "ministry of engagement" where the congregation actually interacts with those receiving the services. We need to get to know people, understand their circumstances, be present to them, and be Christ in their midst.

I encourage all congregations to move beyond missional gestures (which "do good" and make us feel good) to finding at least one "ministry of engagement." In a ministry of engagement, the congregation not only provides resources for those with specific needs, but also has direct contact with those being served. This approach fosters the building of relationships with people so that they may come to know the love of Christ,, engages our hands and feet rather than just our pocketbooks, and helps us to grow in our understanding of the needs of those in our community so that we might address both mercy and justice issues. For example, a new church in Austin, TX invites the women from a neighboring strip club to have dinner with them once a week. These women find a welcoming attitude, a good meal, and the opportunity to make new friends who know Jesus as a joy in their lives.

A ministry of engagement will change our lives as well as the lives of others.

Coaching the Congregation in Service

When coaching the congregation in the area of service, all of these observations come into play. The goal is two-fold:

- To help the congregation consider how it might support the development of disciples who are engaged in service as a personal ministry using their gifts and passions.
- To assist the congregation in identifying opportunities for transforming their community.

The Graduate School of Ministry

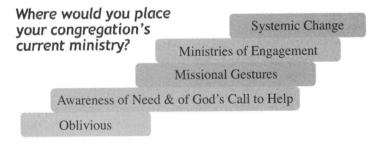

Where would you place your congregation's current ministry?

Systemic Change

Ministries of Engagement

Missional Gestures

Awareness of Need & of God's Call to Help

Oblivious

The Graduate School of Ministry, diagrammed above, is a helpful guide for congregations seeking to live into the mission of "make disciples of Jesus Christ for the transformation of the world." The end goal is to change the systems that create the needs that churches so often try to address in specific ministries.

However, most churches follow some form of the flow addressed above, so let's consider some of the ways a congregation can move to the next level of ministry.

Moving to the Next Level

To help develop an **awareness of the needs** in the community and God's call for your congregation to help, you might consider:

Preaching: My colleague, Jeff Stiggins, had just finished preaching for a local congregation on the theme of discipleship, which included the idea that serving others was part of our commitment as disciples. As he greeted people at the door following worship, one elderly gentleman shook his hand and said "I just want to know when the rules changed. I've attended this church for 50 years and nobody has ever said anything about an expectation that we should be serving others."

I doubt that that is entirely true, but apparently the theme of serving others has not been a major focus.

It should be.

Teaching: There are, of course, lots of great Bible study materials related to serving others. As part of the Christian Education support offered to the discipleship ministries of your congregation, it is recommended that courses in service be included. For example, there are some excellent books that could be studied:

> *Servolution: Starting a Church Revolution through Serving,* Dino Rizzo, Zondervan, 2009 (A great resource to get people excited about serving).

> *Outflow: Outward-focused Living in a Self-focused World,* Steve Sjogren and Dave Ping, Group Publishing, 2006 (5 weeks' of devotions/reflections and group discussion guide)

> *The Externally Focused Church,* Rick Rusaw and Eric Swanson Group Publishing, 2004 (This book quickly became a classic!)

> *When Helping Hurts: How to Alleviate Poverty Without Hurting the Poor...and Yourself,* Steve Corbett and Brian Fikkert,, Moody Publishers, 2009 (A great book on understanding poverty)

> *What Every Church Member Should Know about Poverty,* Bill Ehlig and Ruby K. Payne, Ph.D., aha! Process Inc., 1999 (Lots of great insights—a must read for mission teams)

Clarity about service as an element of discipleship: I recommended previously (From Membership to Discipleship chapter) that a covenant be used for new members. This should include a commitment to service beyond the local church. I also think that it is important that a membership class include an introduction to serving others and identifying each person's gifts for ministry.

Community demographics: A demographic study is a great resource for helping leaders in your congregation become aware of the needs in the surrounding community. There are several companies that provide this service (MissionInsite, Percept). I use MissionInsite regularly. This tool provides, in addition to the general demographic information, the ability to do "opportunity scans" identifying people groups (mosaic groups), household types, and areas of poverty. The new Quad report, in addition to identifying religious trends in an identified area, includes identified needs for particular communities.

Community interviews: Demographic studies are very helpful, but nothing beats "boots on the ground" for getting to know the community. I recommend that the church conduct community interviews:

Getting to know the community….personally! Interviews with community leaders are an excellent way to uncover where the congregation can build bridges into the community.

Who might be helpful to interview? Think of persons who would be able to give you insights into community trends and needs. Such persons in your community might include:

- Mayor
- Councilmen/women
- Police Chief
- Fire Chief
- Homeowners Association
- Realtors

- School principals
- Hospital administrator
- Social Service agencies
- Pastors of other congregations
- Chamber of Commerce
- Neighbors in your community

Praying for the community: Just do it!

- Include community needs in corporate prayers during worship.
- Include community needs in the prayer requests printed in bulletins or church newsletters.
- Send email blasts for prayer when specific needs come up in the community.
- Encourage your congregation to include the needs of the community in their daily prayer time.
- Conduct prayer walks around the community and pray for people and identified needs.
- Canvass your neighborhoods and invite neighbors to share prayer requests.

Celebration of service during worship: It's a pretty standard practice for congregations to celebrate the youth summer mission experience. For the churches I served, we would consecrate the team prior to the trip and allow time in worship for the youth to share about their experiences after they return.

I think the giving of ourselves in service is worthy of celebration when it's a major event or a team doing a local service project or even a family/individual that has made a difference in the community through serving others.

These celebrations demonstrate that the congregation values service and they witness to the variety of types of service people can do. It's a win-win.

The level of ministry I describe as **missional gestures** is an important step in the development of maturing missional congregations. Missional gestures begin to move us from "awareness" to "support" of the needs in the community. These gestures usually require little actual contact with those being served and as a result, little or no relational connection is made. Some of the ways congregations connect with the community through missional gestures include:

Facility Use: It is common practice and a great witness in the community for congregations to provide facilities for community service organizations like the Boy/Girl Scouts, Alcoholics/Narcotics Anonymous, and local support groups. Most of the time there is no actual relationship between those participating in the groups and those in the congregation.

Special Offerings: Local service organizations are always in need of resources (both monetary and physical goods) to support their ministries. Congregations often build in budget line items for support or take special offerings—either financial or specific items (food, socks, underwear, clothing, diapers, etc.).

Community Meals: Many congregations I work with provide a weekly meal for the needy/lonely/homeless in the community. Usually these are supported through donations by local businesses and prepared and served by volunteers.

Partnerships: One of the often-overlooked opportunities for serving the community is that of partnering with local service organizations and even other churches. One local community I worked with had several religious centers along the same stretch of road about 3 miles long. Each of them (United Methodists, Lutherans, Catholics, Presbyterians, Baptists, Muslims, and Mormons) were offering some form of a food pantry to serve the needy in the community. Someone had the brainstorm to pool their resources and create one location for connecting with the community that was supported by all the rest. What a concept!

Churches don't *all* have to provide *every* possible service. Partner!

The next level of ministry is what I call **Ministries of Engagement**. These acts of service move us from passively contributing to the support of those actually doing "hands-on" ministry to being engaged in hands-on ministry. This is the level of ministry through which relationships are formed, needs are more deeply understood, and opportunities for transforming our communities are identified.

Examples of Ministries of Engagement include:

- Tutoring in the local elementary school
- Teaching an ESL (English as a Second Language) group
- Mentoring a middle/high school student
- Adopting a local school
- Providing a weekly meal for the homeless and lonely in the community
- Providing support groups for those in life crises
- Providing an addiction support ministry (Celebrate Recovery)
- Ministry to fire victims

The final level of ministry is that of being involved in changing the systems that produce so many of the needs in our communities. As Joseph Daniels and Christie Latona write in *The Power of Real*:

> *No matter what the issue (homelessness, drugs, crime, etc.) the trans-formation process is started as some entity in the public sector begins organizing people for change. And the best entity to do this is the one that has or should have divine vision—the church.*[6]

Moving Disciples Toward Ministry

As a general pattern for helping people grow in maturity in service in the community, we recommend the following three levels:

- Expose Level: This is the entry level for engaging disciples in service to the community. It is usually a one-time event with no long-term commitment by the disciple. Activities in this level are designed specifically to give the disciple a "taste" of serving. For example, congregations all across the country are conducting occasional "Service Sunday" experiences. In place of the traditional worship service, these congregations do service as worship. Usually the participants go out in teams and are provided with a variety of low-risk service activities. This is often followed by a celebration gathering where stories are shared.

- Experience Level: This level of commitment is still fairly low, but it includes a longer-term commitment, with the disciple being engaged multiple times in a ministry to the community. This level provides the opportunity for hearts to begin changing as people begin to discover the blessing of serving others. For example, some congregations take on the building of a Habitat House. The congregation raises the funds to support the project, and then over the course of many months teams from the church gather to do the actual construction.

- Engage Level: This is a high commitment type of service in the community. Disciples are serving regularly. They are making this service a high priority in their lives. They also begin to mobilize others to support the ministry. For example, congregations across the country are discovering the difference they can make through an "adopt a school" focus of engaging the community. Through these programs, members often commit to provide tutoring for students or to serve as mentors for students over the course of many months.

Let's consider the image of a funnel as a way to frame the discussion and further identify how the congregational leadership might structure a supportive process for developing service to the community.

PERSONAL DISCOVERY AND MISSIONAL ON-RAMPS

Let's start at the top. The wide part of the funnel is the entry point into a life of service. The idea is not just to get people involved in doing some kind of service, but to have them engaged in the service for which God has "wired" them and for which they have a passion.

As part of the discipleship process, most congregations find it helpful to have some form of discovery during which participants learn about their spiritual gifts, their passions, their talents or abilities, their personalities, and their life experiences, all of which contribute to understanding how God might employ them in meaningful service. The two most utilized discovery processes are *SHAPE* inspired by Rick Warren (Saddleback)[7] and *Network* from Willow Creek.[8]

But it takes more than just learning about "wiring." I encourage congregations to provide a variety of entry-level mission/service experiences that disciples can "try on" and see how they fit. We call these "missional on-ramps." There are a variety of ways these can be created. For example:

- Some congregations build a mission component into their small group structure. Each small group is encouraged to take on a monthly mission experience. These do not have to be risk-taking ministries at this point. One group in my last appointment served ice cream to families at a Give Kids the World once a month. They had a great time, made a difference, and were introduced to the joy of serving others.

- Many congregations have ministry partnerships with community organizations. Members are encouraged to serve once a month in any of the ministries as a way of exploring how God might employ their gifts. For example, serving in a community food pantry or serving a meal to the homeless at a local shelter are the types of activities being described.

- A third practice gaining significant popularity is for the entire congregation to have a mission experience day in place of the traditional Sunday worship service. The congregation gathers and prays, then goes out to serve the community together, and finally comes back to celebrate how they saw God at work. It is a great community-building experience for both the congregation and the community being served. There have even been examples of entire districts scheduling a "mission/service Sunday."

Questions for Leaders and Coaches Related to Personal Discovery and Missional On-Ramps:

- How do you encourage the engagement of your congregation in acts of service and mission through your preaching and teaching?
- What training is in place to guide your disciples through a process of discernment in their "wiring" for ministry?
- How do you introduce your congregation to the array of opportunities to be involved in service/mission?
- Describe your theological perspective on the relationship between service (good works) and piety (holy living).
- How have you structured "on-ramp" opportunities for those exploring the types of service that might be the best fit?
- What partnerships have you established with other churches, social service organizations, and local missions?
- In what ways do you lift up and celebrate the engagement of your congregation in service during corporate worship?

COMMUNITY SERVICE AND MISSION OPPORTUNITIES

As the funnel begins to narrow, we reach the next level of involvement. This involves more commitment on the part of the disciples. For example:

- Some congregations have teams that are engaged in a variety of community projects. The church might support a Habitat for Humanity project, provide home repairs for the elderly, or have yard clean-up for single parents. One congregation I worked with helped those who had been cited for non-compliance with city ordinances.

- Congregational mission trips are included at this level of commitment. Most congregations offer some type of annual mission trip (sometimes several) through which disciples can be connected to a more intense mission experience. Some of these are stateside and others are overseas in focus. While all of these experiences help people in practical ways, the ones who often gain the most from the experience are those who participate on the team. This is often the entry point to understanding the significant needs that surround us, to say nothing of the personal impact that mission trips have on our own spiritual journeys.

For the past several years, I have been leading and supporting short-term mission teams in the Caribbean (primarily Jamaica). I know. It's tough duty, but someone has to do it! One of the most common responses from participants on the mission teams is, "I know we helped people this week, but we got so much more out of this experience than they did!" There is nothing like some "hands-on" experience to help people see the impact of the gospel message "with skin."

An important distinction needs to be made at this point. Many congregations are engaged in making a difference through what I call "missional gestures." Ad discussed previously, missional gestures are things we do to support the needy in the community without getting personally involved. For example, the following is a listing of the activities of one church I worked with recently:

- Cuban Mission
- Children's Home
- Good Samaritan
- Interfaith events

- Food bank
- 12-step programs
- Adopt a Child/Family
- Meals on Wheels
- Cooperative feeding
- Disaster relief
- Mentoring (elementary school)
- Operation Christmas Child
- Grief Share
- Neo-natal mission
- Alcoholics Anonymous
- Backpacks
- Quilting
- Miscellaneous collections for community needs
- Scouts
- Youth missions

Wow! Twenty different ministries that are supported by this medium-sized congregation! They were supporting a lot of good ministries in the surrounding community. But as we explored the list, it became clear that in only a couple of instances were any of the people from the congregation actually involved in any way in the lives of the people to whom they were ministering. This congregation provided space, collected supplies, raised money, and served meals. But they didn't get to know anyone they were serving. They didn't build any connections to the love of Jesus that motivated the support provided. They didn't have any better understanding of the issues surrounding the needs. But they felt good about themselves and their faithfulness. That's what missional gestures are about.

Now, I don't want to suggest that the congregation should not provide support for these ministries. These are good things and worthy of our support.

What I *do* recommend is that every congregation have what I call a "ministry of engagement." As you may recall, this is where the people actually become engaged in the lives of those being served, where they witness personally to the love of Jesus by their actions, where they get to know people personally, and where they invite people to discover the love of Jesus for themselves.

The impact of ministries of engagement, in contrast to missional gestures, is dramatic. For example, at one church I served we provided a weekly meal for the homeless and lonely. All of the food was donated by local businesses and prepared by our church members. There was no shortage of volunteers to cook and serve the meal. It started out as what I would call a missional gesture. We cooked and served. The homeless came and ate. There was little to no interaction.

We then made a commitment as leadership and staff for that congregation that we would participate in the weekly meal, but not as cooks or servers. Some of us would eat the meal provided and sit at the tables with the participants and begin to build relationships.

We met some of the most amazing people! Some were highly educated and others had dropped out of school and life. Some were in need because of catastrophes life had thrown at them. Others had simply chosen to opt out of a more traditional lifestyle.

As we shared week after week, relationships began to form. We would greet each other out on the streets. Some of the participants began to feel so welcome that they started coming to worship and other activities. Those relationships began to open other doors to serve this group. I became the ex-officio chaplain for the group and was called upon to help those who were in need of medical care, to provide for those who lost all their meager belongings, and to pray for them in times of difficulty.

When I moved to my next appointment, the homeless group presented me with a brand-new white shirt as a thank you gift. It is a memory I still treasure.

A couple of months after I moved to my new appointment, which was about 150 miles away, Joyce (one of the homeless group) showed up in worship. As she came forward to receive communion, she took my hand and said, "I just wanted to see how they were treating our preacher." Following worship I tried to catch her at the door to the sanctuary, but she was already on her bicycle riding away.

Never underestimate the impact you might have through sharing your life in a serving ministry!

Questions for Leaders and Coaches Related to Community Service and Mission Opportunities:

- How do you identify the needs and opportunities for service in your local community?
- What types of community service and/or missions does your congregation support?

- Describe the community outreach activities of your congregation in both missional gestures and ministries of engagement.
- What opportunities do you provide for short-term mission experiences, stateside and/or overseas?
- What is your goal for involvement in short-term mission experiences?
- How do you process the experiences of those participating in community service and short-term missions?

PERSONAL MISSIONS

The third level (narrow) of the funnel represents the discovery of a calling to a personal ministry. This is really the goal for maturity as a disciple of Jesus Christ.

One of the challenges congregations face is helping people understand the scope of things that fall into the category of personal missions. For example, I think each of the following qualifies:

- Providing transportation for the elderly in the community going to the doctor
- Serving in a local soup kitchen
- Taking care of an elderly neighbor's lawn
- Preparing a meal for the family of a neighbor experiencing illness
- Volunteering at a local hospital
- Tutoring at a local school
- Providing childcare for a neighbor in the hospital
- Serving as a Stephen Minister to those in crisis in your community[9]
- Mentoring a group of middle-school boys or girls

You get the picture! This is certainly not an exhaustive list.

One of the questions churches struggle with is how to measure the overall effectiveness of the process of personal engagement in ministry within a congregation. The reason this is important is that it helps congregations know if what they are doing is moving people toward maturity.

Some congregations use a service card that is placed in the offering plate during worship to track their progress. Others have members move a rock from one bowl to another if they have been engaged in at least one hour of service beyond the congregation. Again, we want to emphasize that the tracking is really for the church to determine the effectiveness of the process.

> ### Questions for Leaders and Coaches Related to Personal Missions:
>
> * How do you encourage the development of a personal mission/ministry for disciples in your congregation?
> * How do you celebrate the involvement of people in living out their calling to serve?
> * What tools do you use to measure the effectiveness of your system for developing a culture of service?

Diagnosing the Level of Service

This dimension of the life of a congregation is one of the most difficult in which to get any concrete data for analysis. Most congregations do not have any statistical measure related to service.

Some congregations (e.g. those in the Florida Conference of the UMC) measure the number of people in the congregation who perform at least one hour of service beyond the church each week. A couple of examples of measurement tools were noted previously. The purpose is to measure the effectiveness of the system of service in encouraging participants to engage in personal ministry.

Communication Tools: A review of several months' of congregational newsletters, worship bulletins, and the website gives a quick insight into the focus of the congregation on service and missions.

Interviews/Focus Groups: Discussions with individuals and/or focus groups will give great insight into the types of service/mission offered by the congregation and a deeper understanding about the level of engagement.

Real Discipleship Survey: This tool is designed for both individual use and as a congregational survey. It highlights the maturity level of individuals in several areas of the discipleship journey, including Service. This tool is available from www.emc3coaching.com. For congregational use, the survey is taken by a representative group and then averaged in each of the dimensions of discipleship as an indicator of the level of maturity for the congregation as a whole.[10]

Congregational Survey: The measurement of service practices as perceived by the congregation is part of a more comprehensive survey of congregational health. This is offered as both a pdf download and in a Survey Monkey format which gives an analysis (www.emc3coaching.com)[11]

Leadership Team Assessment: This document (available from www.emc3coaching.com) is a set of questions for local church leadership teams to consider. The practices of hospitality, worship, discipleship, service, and generosity are all included.[12]

Most of these and other tools are available in *Tips, Tools, and Activities for Coaching Church Leaders,* our companion resource for *Shift.* (See www.mc3coaching.com)

Getting Started: Platform Stuff

In my work with congregations I have found a variety of what I call "critical components" that need to be in place to develop an effective culture of service. These do not comprise the service process but need to be in place in order for the process to be effective.

Identify Acts 1:8 Opportunities

Acts 1:8 gives a paradigm for thinking about ministry to the world around us. In this approach, Jerusalem represents the people in the existing community of faith. What are the needs of that group? Judea represents the people most like the existing community of faith but are not being reached by the congregation with any significant success. What would it take to make a stronger connection? Samaria represents the people in the community who are very different from those represented in the congregation (language, culture, lifestyle, etc.). What would it take to build bridges with these groups?

Provide Missional On-Ramps

To help people discover the joy of being involved in service to others it is helpful to provide "missional on-ramps," easy, low-commitment ways for members of the congregation to become involved. For example, small groups might be encouraged to participate together in a monthly mission project or service opportunity. The leadership of the congregation might arrange for a monthly community service project. These are also a great opportunity for building relationships with those in the community.

Encourage Vocational Exploration

One of the ways a congregation can help foster a culture of service is to help members discover how God has wired them for service. The *SHAPE Workshop*[13] offered to your congregation is one way to do this. Many congregations offer spiritual gifts classes and inventories. Others make this a focus of their new member classes. Encourage the congregation to try out a variety of ways to serve based on what they have discovered about themselves. It is most helpful if there is actually some conversation about what people are learning about themselves and the community they are serving.

Cultivate Community Discovery

One of the greatest surprises for congregations/congregational leadership comes when they begin to discover who actually lives in the community around them. MissionInsite is a great resource for starting this process of discovery. In addition to providing general demographic information, MissionInsite helps you understand the characteristics of the people groups living in your community (Mosaic), identify opportunities for ministry, and target specific age groups for ministry.[14]

It has also been found to be very helpful for congregations to interview community leaders (police chief, fire chief, school principals, mayor, chamber of commerce, realtors, etc.). Asking about the needs of the community from the perspective of these people in the know puts a face on the demographic information. In addition, it creates a lot of good will with the community, but only if you do something with what you learn. A Community Interview Form is available at www.emc3coaching.com.[15]

Create a System for Helping People Discover and Make Their Kingdom Contribution

Many congregations are finding it helpful to build a system for helping members connect their individual gift mix to opportunities for ministry. Some have put together a listing of opportunities with a short description, level of commitment, and possible spiritual gifts that would be helpful. Others have provided this on their website. Some congregations have discipleship coaches who help members of the congregation explore options based on their gifting.

Celebrate Service

One of the most effective ways of encouraging a culture of Service is to celebrate those who are doing it. Worship is a great place for this to happen. Having a service witness just prior to the offering is a way of acknowledging that our offering includes our time and talents as well as our financial resources. Invite people to share their story about making a difference through service. People connect to stories and may be inspired to see how they can make a difference as well.

Track Service

It is suggested that all congregations track the number of people engaged each week in at least an hour of Service, which can be any way that people have met the needs of someone beyond the local church. This is actually a tool to help the local church track its progress, to see if it is heading in the right direction. It has been said that we "tend to get what we measure." If the goal is to impact our communities, wouldn't it be helpful to know if we are making progress?

Suggested Resources for Coaches and Congregations Related to Service:

- *Servolution: Starting a Church Revolution through Serving*, Dino Rizzo, Zondervan, 2009
- *Outflow: Outward-focused Living in a Self-focused World*, Steve Sjogren and Dave Ping, Group Publishing, 2007
- *S.H.A.P.E.: Finding and Fulfilling Your Unique Purpose for Life*, Erik Rees, Zondervan, 2006
- *The Externally Focused Church*, Rick Rusaw, Group Publishing, 2004
- *MissionInsite* (demographic study), www.missioninsite.com
- *When Helping Hurts: How to Alleviate Poverty Without Hurting the Poor...and Yourself,* Steve Corbett and Brian Fikkert, Moody Publishers, 2009
- What Every Church Member Should Know About Poverty, Bill Ehlig and Ruby K. Payne, Ph.D., aha! Process, Inc., 1999

shift 5:

"Survival Mentality" to Generosity

"The generous will themselves be blessed,
for they share their food with the poor."
Proverbs 22:9

"In everything I did, I showed you that by this kind of hard work we
must help the weak, remembering the words the Lord Jesus himself said:
'It is more blessed to give than to receive.'"
Acts 20:35

"Earn all you can, save all you can, give all you can."
John Wesley, founder of Methodism

Consider the following…it is a real-life encounter with a medium-sized congregation. The names have been changed, of course, but you could probably name it from any one of many experiences.

Loveland UMC is a "county seat" congregation that has been in existence for nearly 100 years. For the past several years, the congregation has been in significant decline according to all the normal statistics (worship participation, professions of faith, participation in small discipleship groups, and giving). When the financial situation became the driving factor, the district supervisor suggested that the church engage in a consultation process to see what possibilities existed for moving into a more sustainable future.

While the consultation process covered the full spectrum of congregational life, in the area of financial support the following factors came to light:

- The congregation had experienced a decline in giving of 50% over the past ten years. There was a corresponding loss of worship participation during the same time frame, but slightly less dramatic.

- The average giving per worshiper had remained consistent, and in some years had shown a slight increase.

- The average giving per worshiper was at a level of approximately $1250 per year.

- A significant percentage of the congregation indicated in a Discipleship Growth Survey that they were tithers, and many said that they gave beyond the tithe.

- The church has "borrowed" from discretionary funds and an endowment to meet operating expenses for the past 3 years.

- The preschool run by the church operates at a loss and the congregation makes up the difference. The church also provides facilities, utilities, and custodial staff at no charge.

- Slightly over 20% of the revenues for this congregation come from "rental" income committed by outside organizations using the church facilities.

Observations about Generosity

All or significant portions of this scenario are played out in congregations all across the country, creating an unsustainable financial future for many mainline congregations.

When this happens there is a common response by congregations that is impacted little by location, brand, size, ethnic composition, or theological perspective. It is called "survival mode."

When we are threatened, as human beings and as churches, our survival instinct kicks in and we start putting up our defenses. We begin to "circle the wagons," to use an early American metaphor.

When this happens we start chopping at the budget. Usually the first thing to go is our mission support (both local and missional giving). Then we start to cut back on outreach activities (all the things that we do to engage the community). We start to focus on taking care of our members. We limit Vacation Bible School participation to the children from our church in order to reduce costs. We stop mailing newsletters to those who have missed church. We let the regular maintenance of our facilities and landscaping lapse. We cut the programming budgets for youth and children.

In short, we focus on staying afloat financially and taking care of our own. And this, of course, begins a cycle of diminishing returns.

This is complicated by what Lovett Weems calls the "Death Tsunami."[1] The bottom line is that the strongest financial supporters in many congregations will no longer be with us in the next few years and this will significantly impact the financial base for many congregations. Weems calls for a "financial reset" that must take place if congregations are to be sustainable in the future.

While congregations focus on "survival" techniques, rent their facilities to outside groups, take special offerings or hold rummage sales to make up for financial shortfalls, cut staff and limit ministries, the very thing the church is called to do, make disciples, goes by the wayside.

While Lovett Weems is right and churches do need a financial reset, by this he means adjusting the financial baseline to a more realistic and sustainable level. I am not sure the answer is to circle the wagons. I think the answer is spiritual.

Generosity is about the spiritual discipline of living a life with margins (i.e. living on less than one earns) in order to be a blessing to others. Maturity in the area of generosity is NOT the tithe, although for most people in our congregations this would be a huge step forward. While the biblical standard for giving has been the tithe, or 10% of our income, maturity is about moving beyond the tithe, living on less, and giving more to make a difference in our world.

Yet, one of most significant discoveries in ministry was that the church cannot just state the biblical standard of a tithe and expect people to live into that level of generosity. They simply are not able.

Consider the following insights based on current research[2] and my experience working with a wide variety of congregations:

- 82% of people in our American culture report feeling anxious about money.
- 65% of families live paycheck to paycheck.
- 32% of families can't cover a $5,000 emergency.
- 63% of families don't pay off credit cards monthly.
- 53% of families have less than $25,000 in retirement savings.
- The average mainline churchgoer gives 3% or less of their income to the church.
- Most churches designate less than 5% of their budget to serving the community or engaging in mission beyond the church.

- People spend 12–18% more when purchasing with credit cards than when using cash.

- The average family in American culture carries in excess of $15,000 in credit card debt, not including mortgage and car payments.

- The use of money is a difficult conversation for most congregations—people would rather talk about anything but money.

- There is a prevailing idea that all churches do is talk about money, when in fact most pastors seem to avoid the topic when possible.

- A majority of churches do a minimal job of conducting a stewardship campaign and a relatively small percentage provide any discipleship training around the theme of biblical financial principles.

Let's be really clear. Working with a congregation in the area of generosity can be really touchy. However, it is often a critical area for the spiritual development of disciples and support of essential ministries. The following are some areas where the coach can provide some clarity and a non-anxious presence. As in all coaching, asking the powerful questions can open the congregation to some significant insights.

A Theology of Generosity

We are called to be a generous people because our God is a generous God. Everything we have, everything we are, is a gift from God. It belongs to God and is entrusted to our use. Part of our responsibility is to use what God has provided, not just to meet our own needs, but also to meet the needs of those less fortunate.

This is true for us as individuals. It is also true for congregations.

We have been blessed to be a blessing.

The biblical standard for being a blessing is a tithe (10%) of our resources. I believe that this is the *minimum* standard, even though this level of giving would be a stretch for most Christians. Generosity means that we will live on less than what God has provided in order to bless others more.

Practicing generosity as a lifestyle frees us from our dependence on finding our security in "stuff" and from being enslaved by our creditors so that we can have more stuff. The Word is really clear that it is hard to experience the blessings of God when we're having trouble paying the bills for the things we couldn't afford.

Giving generously is not a way to get something in return, although I believe that God will generously provide for all our needs. The idea of giving in order to receive is not biblical. Generosity is motivated by God's grace, not the expectation of getting something in return.

Sometimes we seem to forget that our giving patterns are a spiritual issue. People spend where their hearts lead them. That may mean that the spending is all about them and becomes what is called "Affluenza" by several authors (e.g. Adam Hamilton in *Enough*)[3]—a combination of materialism and consumerism. Or it may mean that they set aside the biblical tithe (10% of their income) and beyond in order to be a blessing to others. It is all a matter of the heart.

While the annual stewardship campaign with some mention of tithing seems to be the standard approach to getting the "heart" right, the reality is this is not enough in our culture. The truth is that people don't know how to use their resources in God-honoring ways. It is not enough to tell them God's minimum standard is the tithe; we have to show them how to get there.

In my last appointment in the local church, we realized that the standard "preaching about the tithe" wasn't sufficient. We decided to offer Dave Ramsey's *Financial Peace University*,[4] starting with a group of about 10 persons. Over the course of 12 weeks, these families (couples and singles) eliminated around $70,000 worth of debt. At the end of our first year of teaching people about the biblical principles of financial management, the giving level of the congregation increased about 15%. We credited much of that to helping people learn how to use money God's way.

There are a variety of excellent resources to assist your congregation in this process:

Resources for Teaching

There is a growing collection of excellent small group tools for teaching people how to become financially healthy, biblically speaking. After looking over most of these, it seems to me that the basic message is quite similar, but the style, tone and mode of presentation vary considerably. Leaders might want to explore several resources and decide which of them best fits their context and needs.

Financial Peace University: With wide appeal to both churched and unchurched persons struggling with out-of-balance finances, Financial

Peace University is part of the wide array of resources offered by Dave Ramsey. In addition to radio, TV, and community event formats, there is a 13-week video series designed for small group use in congregations. Ramsey approaches financial peace from a biblical perspective. For information go to: http://www.daveramsey.com/fpu/home/.

Journey to True Financial Freedom Seminar: This is the most popular church seminar sponsored by Crown Financial Ministries. Crown continues to develop a variety of resources for different contexts and learning styles. For information go to: www.crown.org

Good Sense Budget Course: Willow Creek Church says that perhaps this six-hour course should have been named, "Principles and Practices for God-honoring Money Management." It teaches biblical principles of money management and basic tools for implementing them in daily life. For information go to: http://www.goodsenseministry.com/.

Managing Our Finances God's Way: Part of Saddleback's Focus Series, developed in partnership with Crown Ministries, Purpose Driven Ministries and Pastor Rick Warren offer this seven-week, video-based, small group study on biblical financial management to be used either individually or in a small group setting. For information go to: http://www.saddlebackresources.com/en-US/Pastors/Focus/FOCUSFinances/FOCUSFinances.htm.

Generous Giving: A privately funded ministry that seeks to encourage givers of all income levels to experience the joy of giving and to embrace a lifestyle of generosity. They offer a large array of online resources at: http://www.generousgiving.org/. Generous Giving has also sponsored national conventions on cultivating generous giving at which speakers from around the country address the topic. Many speeches are available on video and audio.

Questions for Leaders and Coaches Related to Generosity as a Spiritual Discipline:

- How does your discipleship process encourage maturity in the area of generosity?
- What clear vision is presented to your congregation about what God wants for their lives financially?
- What support is provided to help disciples learn biblical principles of financial stewardship?
- What expectations are communicated to new members regarding the financial commitment to the church?

Preaching about Generosity

It is often referenced that Jesus talked more about money than any other topic, even love. If we are faithful to the Scriptures, we also help people understand the hold money can have on their lives and the freedom of living without the bondage of debt.

Certainly I support the value of an annual stewardship emphasis, but I also believe that preaching about the use of our financial resources should be a more constant fare. This does not mean that we have to do a message on tithing every month! But it does mean that the theme of financial stewardship can be woven into a wide variety of message themes.

Perhaps more important than preaching about what God wants *from* us is preaching about what God wants *for* us (an often quoted insight from Andy Stanley).[5] In a culture where people are valued for what they have, we have a message of being valued for who we are. In a culture where security is found in the stuff we have, we have a message of security found in our relationship with Jesus. In a culture where bondage to creditors is a way of life, we have a message of freedom from bondage.

Questions for Leaders and Coaches Related to Preaching about Generosity:

- How is your congregation encouraged to be generous in supporting ministry through a stewardship campaign?

- What is your congregation's attitude toward preaching about financial stewardship?
- How does your congregation address financial stewardship as a spiritual discipline?

GENEROSITY AS PASTORAL CARE

In my early ministry I bought into the idea that the pastor should not know how much people gave to the church. At the core of this was the possibility that by knowing the giving levels, the degree of pastoral care would be influenced. In other words, I would be more attentive to the needs of those who were the biggest givers.

I have made an about-face on this. I now believe that it is important for the pastor to know the giving levels of every family in the congregation. There are several reasons for this:

- Since the use of financial resources is a spiritual issue, the giving level is one indicator of progress toward maturity as a disciple of Jesus Christ.
- If there is a dramatic change in the giving levels of a family/person, it may be an indicator that there is some pastoral care issue that needs attention.
- A dramatic change in the giving levels of a family/person may be the first indication of an issue between them and the church that needs to be addressed.
- The giving level of a family/person should be part of a semi-annual pastoral conversation about how the church might support their continuing spiritual development.

Questions for Leaders and Coaches related to Generosity and Pastoral Care:

- How is giving tracked?
- At what point is the pastor alerted when there are dramatic changes in giving levels of a family or person?

CELEBRATING GENEROSITY

Congregations have a variety of ways in which they might celebrate the generosity of those supporting the ministries. The most common, of course, is the presentation of the offering as the Doxology is sung and then a prayer of blessing and thanksgiving is offered. Some congregations are more creative in the presentation, with clapping and singing and whooping and hollering in celebration of the faithfulness of God. Your congregation will need to find what works best in your context.

It is important to do more than just receive the offering, no matter what form that takes. For example there is nothing more powerful than the testimony of a disciple who has discovered the blessing of tithing and the difference it is making in his or her life or a witness from a family that has overcome the bondage of debt and is experiencing the freedom to give and bless others.

The offering slot in the worship experience is a great time to recognize those who are giving not only their financial support, but also their time and talents to make a difference in the community.

Testimonies from those whose lives have been impacted by the ministries of the congregation are a great way to help people connect the dots between the gifts they offer and the lives that are changed because of their support.

Of course, celebrating generosity is not limited to acts of worship. A simple handwritten note thanking people for their faithfulness and generosity goes a long way. Taking extravagant givers to lunch to express appreciation is a wonderful gesture and strong motivator.

Questions for Leaders and Coaches Related to Celebrating Generosity:

- How is the celebration of generosity built into the structure of your worship experience?
- What "personal touches" are part of your celebration of generosity?

The Role of Leadership

I sat in a meeting with a group of leaders from a long-established downtown congregation. This team was seeking to move the congregation to the next level in worship participation and ministry. The theme for the evening was extravagant generosity. In the course of discussion about faithful discipleship in this area, the Council Chair made the following statement: "I don't think we should have to tithe anymore because we pay so much in taxes and that is so the government can take care of people."

After a moment of disbelief that someone had actually voiced such an immature thought, especially someone in a significant leadership role, I responded: "Well, Jim (not his actual name), let me just quote a Scripture for you—"Give back to Caesar what is Caesar's and to God what is God's" (Mark 12:17).

At that moment, it became clear to me where many of the congregation's issues were coming from!

It is often said that "as the leaders go, so goes the congregation." I think this is particularly true in the spiritual discipline of generosity.

Congregations are encouraged to make maturity in the discipline of generosity part of the leadership selection process. To be abundantly clear, it goes like this: To be an elected leader in a congregation, the person must be tithing or moving toward a tithe. The spiritual maturity of the congregation is driven by the spiritual maturity of the leadership, including generosity.

This expectation makes great sense when you consider the types of decisions that must be made by the leadership team: How will we best use the resources that God has provided to be about the Kingdom work? What kinds of ministries will accomplish God's purposes for this congregation? Do we invest in caring for ourselves and "our" people, or do we invest in the community around us? What percentage of our resources will we spend on bricks and mortar and programming and what will we spend in our mission to transform the world? How will our facilities be used to support the work God is doing in our community?

These types of questions drive the direction of congregational ministries and impact. Do we really want immature believers making these decisions?

It is also important for the congregation to trust leadership to be open and transparent about the way in which finances are handled. There are a variety of factors at play here. For example:

- Is there a budget built around the needs and vision of the congregation?
- Is the vision communicated clearly during a stewardship campaign, giving people the opportunity to support the vision?
- Are regular financial reports prepared and available to the congregation?

- Is the congregation made aware of financial challenges and what leadership is doing to meet them?

- Are there policies that leadership follows to avoid debt and to avoid spending all resources on themselves?

It is worth noting here that those congregations who have done the work of positive change that has resulted in a more outward-focused mission and ministry are also reaping the benefit of more meaningful support. Very few of the congregations interviewed for *Toward Vitality* (a United Methodist denominational study) reported financial difficulties.[6] These congregations were willing to give generously to a sense of vision and purpose that came from a sense of God's purpose for that congregation within its community.

Diagnosing the Level of Generosity

In addition to the coaching questions described, there are a variety of tools available to assist the coach in determining the level of generosity offered within a congregation. For example:

- *Real Discipleship Survey:* This survey instrument (available from www.emc3coaching.com) is used as both a personal growth instrument and as a tool to survey the maturity levels of the congregation in six dimensions of the discipleship journey, including generosity. The latter is helpful in assisting congregations to see areas of need that might be supported by the congregation.[7]

- *Congregational Survey:* The measurement of giving patterns as perceived by the congregation is part of a more comprehensive survey of congregational health. This is offered as both a pdf download and in a Survey Monkey format which gives an analysis (www.emc3coaching.com)[8]

- *Leadership Team Assessment:* This document (available from www.emc3coaching.com) is a set of questions for local church leadership teams to consider. The practices of hospitality, worship, discipleship, service, and generosity are all included.[9]

- *Readiness 360:* This unique online survey (www.readiness360.org) measures the spiritual intensity, missional alignment, dynamic relationships, and cultural openness of your congregation. Designed to serve as an indicator for readiness to multiply, this is a great resource for measuring church health.[10]

Most of these and other tools are available in *Tips, Tools, and Activities for Coaching Church Leaders,* our companion resource for *Shift.* (See www.emc3coaching.com)

Getting Started: Platform Stuff

Conduct an Annual Stewardship Emphasis

It is common practice in most congregations to have an annual stewardship campaign. This usually is done in the fall and runs 4–6 weeks, ending on Thanksgiving. Some churches have found that the beginning of the year works better for them.

This is a time for focused reflection on the commitment each family/household makes to the ministry of the congregation. There are some excellent resources available to assist in developing such a focus. For example:

- *The New Consecration Sunday Stewardship Program* by Herb Miller (available through Cokesbury)[11]
- *The Grow One Sunday Stewardship Program Online* by Herb Miller (available through Cokesbury)[12]
- *Extravagant Generosity* by Michael Reeves and Jennifer Tyler (available through Cokesbury)[13]
- *Committed to Christ: Six Steps to a Generous Life* by Bob Crossman (available through Cokesbury)[14]

Provide Training in Biblical Financial Principles

Some great resources were noted in this chapter's section on teaching generosity. This needs to be part of the Christian Education offered to support the discipling process.

Connect Generosity to the Vision of the Congregation

People tend to be generous when they believe in the cause. One only needs to look to the outpouring of resources in support of those in need due to a natural disaster (hurricane, tornado, flood, etc.). Give them something to believe in and ask them to help make it a reality.

Practice the Ministry of the Ask

I have never considered myself a fund-raiser. The thought of asking people for money made me very uncomfortable. What I discovered is that people actually enjoy the opportunity to get behind a credible cause. Ask them! Tell the story about the difference their giving will make in the community or in the lives of people. Remember that it's not about the money. It's about the difference!

Practice Transparency

It was my practice as a pastor to be as open as possible about the financial status of the congregation. Each year, the budget was distributed in worship so that everyone could see how the leadership planned to use the resources provided. Each month a financial report was made available to the congregation.

When times were "tight," we held congregational meetings where the leadership shared measures being taken to live within our means.

Set Clear Expectations for Membership

In the chapter titled Membership to Discipleship it was suggested that congregations use a membership covenant. Part of this covenant is the expectation that those choosing to become members (join the team called to serve the community) commit to proportional giving and moving toward a tithe.

People tend to rise to the level of our expectations.

Tithe the Church Budget

The way the congregation handles its finances should be a witness to the faithfulness we seek from our members. As I work with churches across the country, I have discovered that a relatively small percentage of them tithe or give more than a tithe from the resources that are provided to serving those in the community.

My suggestion is that a church start with a commitment to a tithe, and then seek to increase the percentage of giving by 1–3% each following year. This is a significant witness to practicing what we preach.

Suggested Resources for Coaches and Congregations Related to Generosity:

- *The New Stewardship Sunday Commitment Program*, Herb Miller (available through Cokesbury)
- *The Grow One Sunday Stewardship Program Online*, Herb Miller (available through Cokesbury)

- *Extravagant Generosity*, Michael Reeves and Jennifer Tyler (available through Cokesbury)
- *Six Steps to a Generous Life*, Bob Crossman (available through Cokesbury)
- *Enough: Discovering Joy through Simplicity and Generosity*, Adam Hamilton, Abingdon Press, 2009
- *Five Practices of Fruitful Congregations*, Robert Schnase, Abingdon Press, 2007
- *Financial Peace University*, Dave Ramsey
- *Journey to True Financial Freedom Seminar*, Crown Ministries

Leading the Charge
Without Getting Trampled

I want to close by sharing some thoughts about how to put some of the things discussed into practice in your local congregation. Having worked with dozens of congregations related to these Shifts over the past several years, I have discovered that there are some things that will help you move toward greater vitality and effectiveness with great support of the congregation. There are also some things that will sabotage your efforts. So, the following thoughts are provided to help make the journey smoother.

Create a Sense of Urgency

As a general rule, people don't change because it makes sense. People change when it is too painful not to! This does not mean that the congregation has to be so broken that it will try anything to get better. It does mean that when people begin to see new possibilities for vitality, the current way of doing things just won't make sense any more.

One of the best ways I know of to help people see new possibilities is to LET them "see new possibilities." If you want to give people a vision for creating a world-class process for intentional hospitality, take them to a church that is doing this well. If you want to create a vision for providing a life-changing youth ministry, visit a youth ministry that is thriving.

I'm a huge fan of learning from the successes of others. It is my experience that congregations that are doing things well love to share their story and help others achieve new levels of excellence. After all, we really are all on the same Kingdom team. With slightly less impact, providing video witnesses to effective ministries can also stimulate discussions around the possibilities.

Another approach is to share stories, or even let people experience the impact of what is not working well. In one of my appointments to a local church, our "praise and worship service" had reached capacity. While it had been clear to leadership for some time that we were going to need to offer another worship option (we only had one multi-purpose space) we decided to continue worshiping with one worship service in that style and keep adding chairs for a while. We had certainly reached an uncomfortably full situation!

When we began to have people leave because they couldn't find a seat or because it was too crowded, leadership could begin to share the stories and people could connect to their own experience.

The best solution we could come up with was to add a fourth service to our Sunday morning schedule. To accommodate this, we needed to change the worship times for all the existing services. Usually one would expect this to be a very difficult proposition. In this case it was easy. Almost everyone understood why this move was necessary. Only one person wrote me a note that came through the offering plate and read, "stupid, stupid, stupid, stupid, stupid, and about 50 more times." Some had experienced the situation firsthand and others knew the stories. It was simply time to do something different.

Invite Dialogue

I cannot overemphasize the importance of inviting people into the conversation about proposed changes. This is especially true for those who have perspectives different from your own. One of the truths about conflict is that it is not a bad thing. Many congregations strive for what is called an "artificial harmony." I call it "death by niceness"!

If you have ten people share their perspective on any common experience, you will get between 8–10 differing viewpoints. This is a good thing. The differing perspectives will strengthen the final decision, and people will feel like they have been valued.

One of the keys in these discussions is to help people understand both the complexity and depth of the issues under consideration. For most things, other than the routine and mundane, there really is no absolutely clear path. As these discussions take place, it is an opportunity to move from the "What do we want?" or "What do we like?" kinds of questions to a more missional focus like "Where is God already at work?" or "If we were to look through God's eyes, what might we see?"

Another key is to outlaw "parking lot meetings." I realize this is easier said than done. However, giving everyone the opportunity to voice opinions and being clear that only what is discussed in open forum holds any weight will go a long way toward eliminating "parking lot meetings."

Take Baby Steps and Manage the Pace

Change is easier when we are not changing everything at once. Most major changes can be broken down into smaller steps that make them more tolerable.

I have really struggled with this one! One congregation I served had installed a video projection system just prior to my arrival (and after the previous pastor had departed). Knowing the value this would bring to worship (both traditional and contemporary) I wanted to just launch into using it to its fullest capability. However, I listened to some wiser people in leadership who understood that would be too much, especially for our more traditional worship experience. So we started only using the screen for announcements and then rolling it up. After a few months we introduced the use of the projection system for hymns. People loved being able to see the words clearly and not having to hold a hymnal, although they had a choice to do either one since the hymn numbers were projected as well as being printed in the bulletins. A few months later we introduced using the system for prayers and the communion liturgy. At the end of about a year, a group from the traditional service asked why they never got to experience "all the cool stuff" we were doing with the contemporary worship services (videos, images, interviews, etc.). We knew then that it was time to use the system to its fullest capability!

Notice that we gave people time to recover from one change before we introduced another new thing. People need some breathing room between changes to get used to what has already been done.

Communicate Sensitively

When communicating change, people need to know "What is changing?", "What is NOT changing?", "Why are we making the change?", and "How does this impact me?"

In any change that is being made, people are going to experience a sense of loss. Acknowledge the loss openly and show respect for the past. Don't be surprised by an over-reaction and a sense of grief.

Share information over and over and over again. Help people see the continuity of the change with what really matters.

Practice the Art of Framing

Framing is an inevitable process of selective influence over the individual's *perception* of the meanings attributed to words or phrases. In communications framing, it is generally positive or negative. A frame defines the packaging of an element of rhetoric in such a way as to encourage certain interpretations and to discourage others.

One way to package the message when introducing some form of change is to frame it within the vision of the congregation, explaining how the change will help the congregation live more fully into the vision. Another way to frame messages includes the framing of the change within what people value. And still another is, whenever possible, to frame the change as an addition rather than a subtraction.

It is also helpful to frame the message in terms of the next chapter in the story, rather than a radical departure from the past.

In one of the congregations I served, we made the transition from celebrating Communion once a month to celebrating Communion in every worship experience. To do this, we talked about the connection in the early church between Word and Table. We taught about the elements of Communion being a re-presentation of Christ in our midst. We highlighted the sense of the presence of Christ in our midst through the sacraments.

As Communion was introduced as a weekly element in the worship experience, we made participation voluntary. Communion was celebrated during a song/hymn following the message, with a clear connection between the message and the grace extended in communion. People were not directed to the Communion Table by ushers, but were given the opportunity to participate if they chose or to stay seated and share in the song if that was their choice.

Everything possible was done to create a sense of a "holy moment" as people came to the table. The lights were dimmed. Candle altars were arranged at the sides of the sanctuary. The altar rail was open for people to spend time in prayer. And prayer partners were available behind the altar rails to pray with people if requested.

In the contemporary service it was an instant "hit." Nearly the whole congregation began to participate immediately. For our more traditional folk, this element of worship was a bit slower to gain momentum, but very few had strong objections if there were people who wanted this experience weekly.

By the time I moved to the next appointment, it was clear that the new pastor could change just about anything he or she wanted in worship—as long as it wasn't weekly Communion!

Celebrate Early Wins

The change process is fueled by success. When there are successes, even small ones, take time to celebrate them. Help people see the impact of the things that are changing. This will help them to be more open to future changes and create a momentum for moving into the future.

In the Annual Conference where I served in the Center for Congregational Excellence, we had provided a couple of different processes for congregational transformation. In each case, while the process had some really good stuff, people couldn't see that any progress was being made. Congregations would work their way through months of learning and visioning before any difference could be seen. They were designed to get to a big strategic plan.

The problem encountered in congregation after congregation was a lack of momentum. Because all the focus was placed on the end goal, the big picture of the future, the energy for change began to wane.

As I built a new process, now called Shift, I broke it down into smaller steps with shorter-term goals and short-term wins. There was a remarkable difference in the way the processes were perceived. People could see that something better was being created. They could experience the difference that was being made. They could celebrate successes. And it created an energy that led to a much stronger finish when we got to the "big picture" stuff.

Just Get Started!

Don't wait for the congregation to be ready or your calendar to clear before getting started. There is never an ideal time. I encourage you to simply select a Shift, one that resonates with you and your leadership team, and begin addressing the "Getting Started" stuff.

Suggested Resources for Coaches and Congregations Related to Leading the Charge without Getting Trampled

- Leading Congregational Change, Jim Herrington, Mike Bonem, and James Furr, Josey-Bass Publishers, San Francisco, CA, 2000
- Redeveloping the Congregation, Mary Sellon, Daniel Smith, and Gail Grossman, Alban Institute, St. Herndon, VA, 2002
- Leading Change in the Congregation, Gilbert Rendle, Alban Institute, St. Herndon, VA, 1998
- Managing Transitions: Making the Most of Change, William Bridges, Da Capo Press, Cambridge, MA, 2003
- Leading Change, John Kotter, Harvard Business School Press, Cambridge, MA, 1993

Notes

Shift 1: From Fellowship to Hospitality

1. Michael Slaughter, *Momentum for Life,* Abingdon Press, Nashville, TN, 2005, p. 71.
2. Robert Schnase, *Five Practices of Fruitful Congregations,* Abingdon Press, Nashville, TN, 2007, p. 18.
3. Henry Cloud & John Townsend, *Safe People,* Zondervan, Grand Rapids, MI, 1996, pp. 21–24, 143–144.
4. Doug Anderson & Michael Coyner, *The Race to Reach Out,* Abingdon Press, Nashville, TN, 2004, p.55.
5. Steve Sjogren, "94 Community Servant Evangelism Ideas for Your Church," *SermonCentral,* 2011, www.sermoncentral.com.
6. *Walk to Emmaus, The Upper Room,* General Board of Discipleship, www.upperroom.org/emmaus
7. Alan Hirsch, *The Forgotten Ways,* Brazos Press, Grand Rapids, MI, 2006, pp. 133–134.
8. Henri Nouwen, as quoted by Eric Cooter, "21st Century Wells: Christian Community in the Third Place," *Ministry Matters,* March 11, 2013, www.ministrymatters.com.
9. Doug Anderson & Michael Coyner, *The Race to Reach Out,* Abingdon Press, Nashville, 2004, p.14.
10. *Readiness 360,* online congregational survey, 2012, www.readiness360.org.
11. Phil Maynard, "Mystery Visitor Report Form," *Excellence in Ministry Coaching,* 2012, www.emc3coaching.com.
12. Welcoming Congregation Certification, United Methodist Communications, www.umcom.org.
13. Phil Maynard, "Real Discipleship Survey," *Excellence in Ministry Coaching,* 2012, www.emc3coaching.com.
14. Phil Maynard, "Congregational Survey," *Excellence in Ministry Coaching,* 2012, www.emc3coaching.com.
15. Phil Maynard, "Discovering the Possibilities," *Excellence in Ministry Coaching,* 2012, www.emc3coaching.com.
16. Phil Maynard, "Leadership Team Assessment," *Excellence in Ministry Coaching,* 2012, www.emc3coaching.com.
17. Rethink Church & Welcoming, United Methodist Communications, www.umcom.org.
18. Jeff Stiggins, *Behavioral Covenants: Holy Manners,* PowerPoint presentation available at www.emc3coaching.com.

Shift 2: From Worship as an Event to Worship as a Lifestyle

1. Louie Giglio, *Wired For a Life of Worship: Student Edition of The Air I Breathe*, Multnomah Books, Colorado Springs, CO, 2006, p. 48.
2. Matt Redman, "The Heart of Worship," *STLyrics*, www.stlyrics.com.
3. Cathy Townley, *Missional Worship*, Chalice Press, St. Louis, MO, 2011, p. 11.
4. Kim Shockley, *Toward Vitality Research Project Final Report*, General Board of Discipleship, United Methodist Church, 2012.
5. United Methodist Television, United Methodist Communications, www.umcom.org.
6. George Barna, *Growing True Disciples: New Strategies for Producing Genuine Followers of Christ*, WaterBrook Press, Colorado Springs, CO, 2001, p. 59.
7. Dr. Bernice McCarthy, *4MAT*, About Learning Inc., www.aboutlearning.com.
8. Len Wilson & Jason Moore, *Taking Flight With Creativity: Worship Design Teams that Work*, Abingdon Press, Nashville, TN, 2009.
9. Phil Maynard, "Mystery Visitor Report Form," *Excellence in Ministry Coaching*, 2012, www.emc3coaching.com.
10. Phil Maynard, "Real Discipleship Survey," *Excellence in Ministry Coaching*, 2012, www.emc3coaching.com.
11. Phil Maynard, "Congregational Survey," *Excellence in Ministry Coaching*, 2012, www.emc3coaching.com.
12. Phil Maynard, "Discovering the Possibilities," *Excellence in Ministry Coaching*, 2012, www.emc3coaching.com.
13. Phil Maynard, "Leadership Team Assessment Audit," *Excellence in Ministry Coaching*, 2012, www.emc3coaching.com.
14. Phil Maynard, "Worship Survey," *Excellence in Ministry Coaching*, 2012, www.emc3coaching.com.
15. Dave Ferguson, Jon Ferguson, & Eric Bramlett, *The Big Idea*, Zondervan, Grand Rapids, MI, 2007, pp. 17–18.
16. Rethink Church & Welcoming, United Methodist Communications, www.umcom.org.

Shift 3: From Membership to Discipleship

1. *The Book of Discipline of the United Methodist Church—2012*, The United Methodist Publishing House, Nashville, TN, 2012, p. 91.
2. *The United Methodist Hymnal: Book of United Methodist Worship*, The United Methodist Publishing House, Nashville, TN, 1989, p. 14.
3. Greg Ogden, *Transforming Discipleship: Making Disciples a Few at a Time*, IVP Books, Downers Grove, IL, 2003, pp.42–46.
4. Rick Rusaw & Eric Swanson, *The Externally Focused Church*, Group Publishing, Loveland, CO, 2004, p.141.
5. David Kinnaman & Gabe Lyons, *UnChristian*, Baker Books, Grand Rapids, MI, 2007, p. 28.

6. Jim Putman, *Real Life Discipleship: Building Churches that Make Disciples,* NavPress, Colorado Springs, CO, 2010, p.43.

7. Greg L. Hawkins & Cally Parkinson, *Move: What 1,000 Churches Reveal About Spiritual Growth,* Zondervan, Grand Rapids, MI, 2011, p.34.

8. Ibid., p. 55.

9. Ibid., p. 94.

10. *The Upper Room Daily Devotional Guide,* The Upper Room, General Board of Discipleship, United Methodist Church, www.upperroom.org

11. Phil Maynard, "Real Discipleship Survey," *Excellence in Ministry Coaching,* 2012, www.emc3coaching.com.

12. Phil Maynard, "Congregational Survey," *Excellence in Ministry Coaching,* 2012, www.emc3coaching.com.

13. Phil Maynard, "Leadership Team Assessment," *Excellence in Ministry Coaching,* 2012, www.emc3coaching.com.

Shift 4: From "Serve Us" to Service

1. Lovett Weems, *Leadership in the Wesleyan Spirit,* Abingdon Press, Nashville, TN, 1999, pp. 37–38.

2. Rick Rusaw & Eric Swanson, *The Externally Focused Church,* Group Publishing,Loveland, CO, 2004.

3. Lovett Weems, *Leadership in the Wesleyan Spirit,* Abingdon Press, Nashville, TN, 1999, pp. 37–38.

4. Kim Shockley, *Toward Vitality Research Project Final Report,* General Board of Discipleship, United Methodist Church, 2012.

5. Rick Rusaw & Eric Swanson, *The Externally Focused Church,* Group Publishing,Loveland, CO, 2004.

6. Dr. Joseph W. Daniels, Jr. & Christine Shinn Latona, *The Power of Real,* Not Just a Curtain Puller, Washington, D.C., 2011, p. 295.

7. Erik Rees, *S.H.A.P.E.*, Zondervan, Grand Rapids, MI, 2006, pp.37–95.

8. Bruce Bugbee, Don Cousins, & Bill Hybels, *Network,* Zondervan, Grand Rapids, MI, 1994.

9. Stephen Ministries, St. Louis, www.stephenministries.org.

10. Phil Maynard, "Real Discipleship Survey," *Excellence in Ministry Coaching,* 2012, www.emc3coaching.com.

11. Phil Maynard, "Congregational Survey," *Excellence in Ministry Coaching,* 2012, www.emc3coaching.com.

12. Phil Maynard, "Leadership Team Assessment," *Excellence in Ministry Coaching,* 2012, www.emc3coaching.com.

13. Jessica Neely, *SHAPE Workshop,* Excellence in Ministry Coaching, 2012, www.emc3coaching.com.

14. MissionInsite, www.missioninsite.org.

15. Phil Maynard, "Community Interview Form," *Excellence in Ministry Coaching,* 2012, www.emc3coaching.com.

Shift 5: From "Survival Mentality" to Generosity

1. Lovett Weems, "The Coming Death Tsunami," *Ministry Matters*, October 5, 2011, www.ministrymatters.com.
2. Dan Wesley, "The American Family's Financial Turmoil," *Visual Economics*, April 29, 2010, http://visualeconomics.creditloan.com.
3. Adam Hamilton, *Enough*, Abingdon Press, Nashville, TN, 2009.
4. Dave Ramsey, *Financial Peace University*, www.daveramsey.com/fpu.
5. Patrick Johnson, "How to Preach on Money, Stewardship, and Generosity," *Generous Church*, www.generouschurch.com.
6. Kim Shockley, *Toward Vitality Research Project Final Report*, General Board of Discipleship, United Methodist Church, 2012.
7. Philip Maynard, "Real Discipleship Survey," *Excellence in Ministry Coaching*, 2012, www.emc3coaching.com.
8. Philip Maynard, "Congregational Survey," *Excellence in Ministry Coaching*, 2012, www.emc3coaching.com.
9. Philip Maynard, "Leadership Team Assessment," *Excellence in Ministry Coaching*, 2012, www.emc3coaching.com.
10. *Readiness 360*, online congregational survey, 2012, www.readiness360.org.
11. Herb Miller, *New Consecration Sunday Stewardship Program*, Abingdon Press, Nashville, TN, 2001.
12. Herb Miller, *The Grow One Sunday Stewardship Program Online*, Abingdon Press, Nashville, TN, 1999.
13. Reeves & Tyler, *Extravagant Generosity Planning Kit*, Abingdon Press, Nashville, TN, 2011.
14. Bob Crossman, *Committed to Christ: Six Steps to a Generous Life*, Abingdon Press, Nashville, TN, 2012.

Appendix A

"One Anothers" in New Testament

1. Love one another (John 13:34).
2. Depend on one another (Romans 12:5 amp).
3. Be devoted to one another (Romans 12:10).
4. Wash each other's feet (John 13:14).
5. Rejoice with one another (Romans 12:15; 1 Corinthians 12:26).
6. Weep with one another (Romans 12:15).
7. Live in harmony with one another (Romans 12:16).
8. Don't judge one another (Romans 14:13).
9. Accept one another (Romans 15:7).
10. Admonish one another (Colossians 3:16).
11. Greet one another (Romans 16:16).
12. Wait for one another (1 Corinthians 11:33).
13. Care for one another (1 Corinthians 12:25).
14. Serve one another (Galatians 5:13).
15. Be kind to one another (Ephesians 4:32).
16. Forgive one another (Ephesians 4:32; Colossians 3:13).
17. Be compassionate toward one another (Ephesians 4:32).
18. Encourage one another (1 Thessalonians 5:11).
19. Submit to one another (Ephesians 5:21).
20. Bear with one another (Ephesians 4:2; Colossians 3:13).
21. Stimulate love in one another (Hebrews 10:24).
22. Offer hospitality to one another (1 Peter 4:9).
23. Minister gifts to one another (1 Peter 4:10).
24. Be clothed in humility toward one another (1 Peter 5:5).
25. Don't slander one another (James 4:11).
26. Don't grumble against one another (James 5:9).
27. Confess your sins to one another (James 5:16).
28. Pray for one another (James 5:16).
29. Fellowship with one another (1 John 1:7).
30. Don't be puffed up against one another (1 Corinthians 4:6).
31. Carry one another's burdens (Galatians 6:2).
32. Honor one another (Romans 12:10).
33. Instruct one another (Romans 15:14).
34. Prefer one another (Romans 12:10).
35. Comfort one another (2 Corinthians 1:4).

habits · attitudes · skills

Coaching Foundations

This highly interactive and practical 2-day workshop provides the participant with the skills and experiences to engage in effective and helpful coaching conversations with pastors and key lay leadership. These skills are universal in scope and helpful for anyone wishing to strengthen their ability to provide coaching for ministry leadership.

Participants will:

· Understand distinctions between coaching and other partnerships
· Develop a basic coaching skill set
· Create and sustain effective coaching relationships
· Become proficient with a coaching model
· Develop an awareness of coaching ethics

The training event includes both training and practical experiences and includes specific focus on:

· Coaching definition and distinctions
· Coaching skill set (LEARN)
· Coaching models
· Creating the coaching relationship
· Code of ethics
· Coaching competencies
· Coaching practicum
· Coaching applications
· Discern the possibilities for ministry coaching

How do you get
connected to this unique process?

Dr. Phil Maynard
Director

Excellence in Ministry Coaching
drphilm@emc3coaching.com

321-217-6007

Discipleship Coaching

A one-day workshop designed for congregations hoping to strengthen the process of developing mature disciples of Jesus Christ. With a focus on individual development, clear discipleship goals, and personal accountability discipleship coaching is the clear choice for partnering with those in your congregation seeking greater maturity in their discipleship journey!

Participants will:

· Understand distinctions between coaching and other partnerships
· Develop a basic coaching skill set
· Become proficient with a coaching model for discipleship coaching
· Learn to utilize a discipleship coaching assessment tool for working
  with disciples in your congregation!

This training is offered through Excellence in Ministry Coaching. All facilitators are trained coaches with a wealth of personal coaching, ministry coaching, and discipleship coaching experience

How do you get
connected to this unique process?

Dr. Phil Maynard
Director

Excellence in Ministry Coaching
drphilm@emc3coaching.com

321-217-6007

habits · attitudes · skills

Discovering the Possibilities

Discovering the Possibilities is a facilitated process designed to assist congregational leaders in understanding the realities of their ministry context or current ministries, and to begin discerning possibilities for their future in ministry. We believe that every congregation has the potential to be faithful and fruitful in ministry. Statistics are clear, however, that this is not the current reality for many of our congregations. Discovering the Possibilities is a process designed to give congregations a realistic sense of what fulfilling their ministry potential might mean.

Data Gathering
Church leaders gather information about the congregation's ministry

Current Realities
The congregation examines its history, current ministry practices, resources and facilities

Ministry Potential
The congregation discerns opportunities for ministry in its community and possibilities for the future

Reporting Findings
The facilitator summarizes the findings and makes recommendations in a written report to the congregation

The Discovering the Possibilities Workshop is a 5-hour event consisting of two parts:

Part A: Current Realities
A series of activities exploring congregational practices, discipleship system, and leadership development

Part B: Ministry Opportunities
Participants examine demographic information for their ministry context. They will then begin to identify mission opportunities and potential connections for community engagement

How do you get connected to this unique process?

Dr. Phil Maynard
Director

Excellence in Ministry Coaching
drphilm@emc3coaching.com

321-217-6007

emc³
excellence
in ministry
coaching
habits · attitudes · skills

From Membership to Discipleship

How can you bring this transformational training to your church or district?

Part 1: Foundations
This session will introduce your discipleship team to a core definition for discipleship, differentiate between discipleship and Christian Education.

Part 2: Movements
Differentiate between membership and discipleship, make observations about the movement toward maturity.

Part 3: Discipleship as a Contact Sport
Explore a variety of discipling relationships, the value of each, and where each fits best.

Part 4: Equipping for Transformation - (Support the Discipling Process)
Discover what types of relationships and educational support work best for supporting disciples.

Part 5: Building an Intentional Discipleship Process
Learning from history, participants identify the key elements of a transformational discipleship process.

How do you get connected to this unique process?

Dr. Phil Maynard
Director

Excellence in Ministry Coaching

drphilm@emc3coaching.com
321-217-6007